PHILOSOPHY AND GRAMMAR

SYNTHESE LIBRARY

STUDIES IN EPISTEMOLOGY,

LOGIC, METHODOLOGY, AND PHILOSOPHY OF SCIENCE

VOLUME 143

PHILOSOPHY AND GRAMMAR

Papers on the Occasion of the Quincentennial of Uppsala University

Edited by

STIG KANGER and SVEN ÖHMAN
Uppsala University

D. REIDEL PUBLISHING COMPANY
DORDRECHT : HOLLAND/BOSTON : U.S.A.
LONDON : ENGLAND

Library of Congress Cataloging in Publication Data

Main entry under title:

Philosophy and grammar.

(Synthese library ; v. 143)
English or German
Includes bibliographical references and index.
CONTENTS: Von Wright, G. H. Humanism and the humanities. – Quine, W. V. Grammar, truth, and logic. – Follesdal, D. Comments on Quine. [etc.]
1. Grammar, Comparative and general – Congresses. 2. Language and logic – Congresses. 3. Semantics – Congresses. I. Kanger, Stig. II. Öhman, Sven, 1935– III. Uppsala. Universitet.
P153.P46 415 80–15692
ISBN 90–277–1091–0

Published by D. Reidel Publishing Company,
P.O. Box 17, 3300 AA Dordrecht, Holland.

Sold and distributed in the U.S.A. and Canada
by Kluwer Boston Inc.
190 Old Derby Street, Hingham, MA 02043, U.S.A..

In all other countries, sold and distributed
by Kluwer Academic Publishers Group,
P.O. Box 322, 3300 AH Dordrecht, Holland.

D. Reidel Publishing Company is a member of the Kluwer Group.

Printed in The Netherlands

TABLE OF CONTENTS

PREFACE

Among the several dozens of symposia held on the occasion of the quincentennial of Uppsala University, there was included one symposium devoted to the theme of 'Philosophy and Grammar'. A selection of the most important papers delivered at this symposium have been collected in this volume.

The papers need no introduction, but the inclusion of two of them in this collection requires a brief comment.

First, the paper by von Wright, although not directly concerned with the central topic of the symposium, has been included because it was the terminating speech of the six parallel symposia (including the symposium on 'Philosophy and Grammar') held by the Humanities Faculty and moreover, because the raison d'etre of the Humanities is analyzed in this paper by a very prominent Swedish-speaking philosopher.

Second, Professor Hintikka was unable to participate. In view of his expertise in the field, we nevertheless requested him to contribute a paper, so to speak, *post factum*. This he very generously did.

We wish to express our sincere appreciation to all who participated and/or helped to carry the sessions through to a successful conclusion. We also wish to extend a special thanks to Professor Roman Jakobson of Harvard University, who assumed the responsibility of General Chairman of the symposium.

STIG KANGER
SVEN ÖHMAN

GEORG HENRIK VON WRIGHT

HUMANISM AND THE HUMANITIES

1. It seems appropriate to start my talk with a few remarks about the two terms which occur in its title. Although both words, 'humanism' and 'humanities', have Latin roots, neither of them has a straightforward equivalent in classical Latin. Cicero uses *studia humanitatis* as a name for the intellectual pursuits best fitted for a gentlemanly education, or for developing what he calls a man's *humanitas*. Reading the historians and the poets was a main ingredient of such studies. In 19th century Germany *humanistische Wissenschaften* established itself as a common name for the historical and philological disciplines. One also speaks of the *humaniora*, in English the Humanities. I think this a useful term. It has, it seems, no very firmly established connotation. Here I propose to use it for the totality of disciplines which study human nature and the achievements of man as a being capable of culture. Then it covers also the social sciences and the broad field of cultural anthropology.

The term 'humanism' too seems to be a 19th century German invention (*Humanismus*). It was originally used for referring to the Renaissance current in literature and scholarship, the representatives of which in Italy had, at the time, been known as *umanisti*. The pursuits of the *umanisti* had meant a revival of interest in the classic Greek and Latin authors. Accordingly, 'humanism', or 'neo-humanism', became a name also for the second return to the ancients in the search of standards of beauty and style which took place in late 18th and early 19th century Germany.

With the humanism both of the Renaissance and of the Enlightenment was also connected a certain view of man, of his potentialities and their proper cultivation. Sometimes this view found articulation in a philosophy, sometimes it existed only as an implicit attitude to life and society. For this value-loaded view too the name 'humanism' has become current. When, for example, one speaks today of an existentialist or of a socialist humanism, what one has in mind is a philosophy of life – related maybe to views entertained by humanists of the Renaissance or by some neohumanists, but independent of a scholarly interest in ancient history or literature. Similarly, when one speaks of the humanism of the Ancients, one is thinking not so much of their contributions to humanistic

S. Kanger and S. Öhman (eds.), Philosophy and Grammar, 1–16.

studies as of a certain philosophic interest in man and concern for human values.

In the title of my paper, 'humanism' refers to an attitude to life, an explicit or implicit philosophical anthropology. By 'the humanities' again I shall understand the scholarly study of man as a being of culture. In spite of this disparity of meaning, there is a connection between humanism and the humanities which is not only historical and accidental but also philosophical and essential. I hope this will be clear from what follows.

2. The life of primitive man is a struggle with nature. Man is, so to speak, at the mercy of his natural environment: immediate supply of food, protection against climatic changes and wild beasts – these are his basic needs. Behind the operation of natural forces man fancies the hand of benevolent or inimical super-natural beings, whom he fears and tries to soothe. The germ of a humanist attitude was laid the moment when man stopped to consider his potentialities in the fight with nature and to vindicate his freedom in face of the gods. In the myth of Prometheus, who taught man the crafts and the use of fire, we see this moment reflected in the folklore of a singularly gifted nation. It was in ancient Greece that the germ was first developed into a rational attitude to man and the world.

It has become tradition to describe early Greek rational thought as a philosophy of nature or even as a proto-science. Its grand idea was the conception of the universe as a *kosmos* or lawful order. 'Nature's law', its *arche* or guiding principle, also applies to man who is a *mikrokosmos*. Health is the natural state of the human body. By a profound medical analogy the good life for man and society was thought of as a state of health, i.e. agreement with the principles governing the kosmos. This, I should say, is the core of the humanist attitude as it appears in Greek culture.

It almost goes without saying that, on this view, natural law does not mean simply a universal regularity in the factual course of events. The law of nature is also a standard to which things must conform in order to be in accord with *their* 'nature'. Applied to human affairs, this means that the good life pursues the natural order of things as an ideal or norm. It is worth noting that the Greek word *physis* like the Latin *natura* and our 'nature' has a double meaning. It means nature in the restricted sense of external reality, but it also means the essence of order of things.

The idea that 'the nature of nature' is a lawful order can rightly be said to constitute the foundation and backbone of what we too should call a 'scientific' view of the world. But the semi-normative understanding of it, characteristic of Greek thought, is not a scientific idea in our sense. The contributions of the Ancients to what we understand by natural science and by humanistic scholarship were not of impressive magnitude. Their great contribution to rational thought was rather the early formation of a humanist attitude. This partly explains why later currents in history which have become known as 'humanist' have almost invariably looked to Greek and Roman antiquity as a source of inspiration and wisdom.

3. During the Christian civilization of the Middle Ages the humanist inheritance of the Ancients was by no means entirely effaced. But times were hardly favourable to its further development. Nature lost its positive value-load and therewith its interest to the inquiring mind. The intellectual energies of man were directed towards the divine, to objects of pure thought beyond the evidence of our senses. It is no accident that some centuries of the Middle Ages came to be a golden age of logic – nor that this noble discipline should, with the turning of the tide in history, have fallen into a disrepute from which it has been rescued only in the last one hundred years.

When viewed against the background of the Middle Ages, the Renaissance – to quote Jacob Burckhardt's famous words – meant a rediscovery of man and of nature. But nature rediscovered was rather different from the *kosmos* of the Greeks. It was not so much a lofty ideal to be imitated by man as a brute force to be subjugated by him. Man, the crown of creation, is 'lord and commander of the elements' – to quote Marlowe's drama about Doctor Faustus. The aim of a science of nature is to make it possible for man to exploit nature's resources and put its forces in the service of human ends.

A prescientific form of this 'Faustian spirit' of Western man is the magic of the Middle Ages and the Renaissance. With the Italian *umanisti*, in particular Ficino and Pico della Mirandola, begins a rationalization of it. In the philosophic program of Francis Bacon this process is consummated. With Bacon's name is associated the slogan 'knowledge is power'. Knowledge, for Bacon, meant in the first place knowledge of the causes of natural events. Causes are found by making experiments. Experimenting means studying the course of events under simplified and controllable and thus in a sense 'artificial' or 'unnatural' conditions. This kind of 'violence on nature' is alien to the typically Greek mind. To Western science it is fundamental. The experimentalist spirit may be said to be the mode of intellectual curiosity most typical of Western man. It had guided the alchemists in the search for the Stone of Wisdom which was supposed to bring power and riches. It made Leonardo dream of the construction of aircraft for the conquest of space. These endeavours had still to wait a few more centuries for their successful fulfilment. Of more immediate reward was Vesalius's vivisection on the tissues of the living body or Galileo's study of the laws of free fall by means of sloping planes – thus artificially 'diluting' the force of gravitation.

Experimentally founded causal knowledge provides the possibility of producing or suppressing events in nature by manipulating their causes. Gearing natural processes for the sake of attaining the desired and avoiding the shunned is of the essence of scientific technology. It would certainly not be right to say that the only or even the main motive force for the erection of the lofty intellectual fabric of modern natural science had been the wish for technological applications. But it is certain that natural science has continued to nourish the dream of a scientific technology in the service of man. With the advent of the great social change called the industrial revolution, this dream has become more and more of a reality with profound effects on human life at all levels.

4. The rediscovery of nature and of man – still to use Burckhardt's characterization of the Renaissance – also posed a new problem. I shall call it the Problem of Man's Place in Nature. For the Greeks this was no problem. The blend of fact and ideal which is characteristic of their conception of the cosmic order tended to slur over problems which become intriguing when the notion of nature's law has developed into that of a factual 'iron necessity' governing the course of all things.

In his so-called 'Oration on the Dignity of Man' the Renaissance humanist Pico della Mirandola had expressed the idea that man, alone among God's creatures, has no fixed place in the great order of things. It is up to man himself to choose his place, what he will be: beast or angel or something in between. In the terminology of mediaeval scholasticism Pico's idea amounts to saying that in man existence precedes essence – a formula for human freedom familiar also from modern existentialism.

Pico also wrote a treatise against astrology. It is false and unworthy of men, he says, to believe that human destiny is predetermined by the constellations of heavenly bodies and other 'signs in the sky'. Astrology, however, was a strong influence at the time, a lingering variety of protoscientific magic. Pico's attack on astrology was met by a counterattack by no less than Johannis Kepler, one of the founding fathers of modern exact science. Kepler was deeply convinced that human affairs depend on the mutual positions of the stars. We may think this a most unscientific view. But, abstracting from the element of superstition in it, this is also a conviction that man *has* a fixed place in the cosmic order, that human affairs too are governed by inexorable laws of the universe. To have this conviction may be to overlook something essential about man. But it can hardly be labelled a superstition. It would be more right to call it an implicit philosophy of man which has been continuously nourished, since the days of Kepler, by the victorious progress of science.

The positions of Pico and Kepler typify two stands on the question of man's place in the world-order.[1] One could call them a *humanist* and a *naturalist* attitude. It goes without saying that the opposition between them is also relevant to the question of the place of the Humanities in the totality of the *Wissenschaften*.

5. Renaissance humanism had acted as a catalyst or midwife for an exact science of nature. This new science, moreover, promised man domination over nature. But it did not teach man the mastery over himself of which Greek humanism may be said to have been in search. The rediscovery of man to which Renaissance humanism contributed was not so much the establishing of a self-searching attitude as the liberation of artistic and intellectual energies from the constraints of received religious authority. It inaugurated a process of secularization which has, since then, been steadily progressing.

Man's search for himself had still to await a new wave in the movement of humanist thought. This wave was the humanism of the Enlightenment. Just as Renaissance humanism belongs in the setting of the troubled times of religious reform, neohumanism must be seen in connexion with the great social upheaval of the French Revolution and the consequent unrest of the Napoleonic era. The lesson taught by the external drama of the time could perhaps be summarized as follows:

Man unleashed from received secular and spiritual authority is a beast, who has to be tamed before he can make proper use of his freedom. The taming of the beast is the education of man to a dignified and enlightened human being. In Germany, the homeland of the humanism of the Enlightenment in much the same sense in which Italy had been the cradle of Renaissance humanism, the two humanist catchwords of the time were *Bildung* and *Erziehung*.

Like their Italian precursors, the German neohumanists looked to the Ancients for their ideals of beauty and culture. But this traditional 'humanist nostalgia' was now coupled with a much more profound classical scholarship and a new understanding of humanity's past. The study of history and languages and human *mores* was placed on a new footing early in the 19th century. Gradually, what we call the social sciences too established themselves on the academic stage.

The humanism of the Enlightenment thus gave origin to a scholarly study of man and his society, deserving the name 'scientific' in the German sense of *wissenschaftlich*. The 19th century is the era of the great classics in the Humanities. Niebuhr, Ranke, and Mommsen were the Copernicus, Kepler, and Galileo of historiography; Wilhelm von Humboldt, Jacob Grimm, and Rasmus Rask those of the study of language; Marx, Durkheim, and Weber those of sociology.

6. The developments which led to the birth of the humanities did not by themselves much affect our views of man's place in nature. A revolutionary impact on these views, however, came from 19th century natural science – chiefly from Darwin and the theory of evolution. The upheaval in ideas brought about by Darwin's theory is comparable only to the effects which the Copernican system and the subsequently emerging view of the infinitude of the universe had had on the human world-perspective two or three centuries earlier.

In the footsteps of Darwinism followed a deterministic naturalism which in many ways can be regarded as a reaction against the libertarian idealism of the era of neohumanism and the French Revolution. The humanities, though born in the atmosphere of idealism could not fail in their growth to maturity to be affected by the prevailing climate of naturalism. The question 'What is man's place in nature?' is from now on paralleled by the question 'How are the humanities related to the natural sciences, the scientific study of man to the scientific study of nature?'

Two confronting positions on this last issue mirror the attitudes of Pico the humanist and Kepler the natural scientist. It is interesting to note that in the two major figures who have most profoundly influenced our understanding of man and society, Marx and Freud, the two attitudes strongly intermingle. It has become the fashion to speak of two Marxes: Marx the humanist who put emphasis on man's possibilities of emancipating himself from exploitation and slavery and of overcoming alienation, and Marx the historical materialist who in the evolution of society saw the working of 'iron laws' concerning the interplay of productive forces and productive relations. It is usual to connect the two attitudes with the young and the mature Marx – and there is *some* truth in this. But the more interesting fact about Marx is that the two attitudes are both present, implicitly, in his work as a whole. Therefore all those for whom Marx continues a source of inspiration – philosophers, social scientists, and the exegetes of various socialist creeds – are likely always to fall back, now on one, now on another of the potentialities inherent in this strangely contradiction-loaded thinker. Something similar holds true of Freud. His theorizing largely follows the pattern of 19th century 'naturalist' medicine and psychology with their implicit determinist view of man. That Freud's insights can be given a very different – and from the point of view of therapy probably much more fertile – interpretation is evident from modern trends in psychiatry and what is nowadays sometimes called 'humanist' psychology.

7. The polarization implicit in these giants of thought is explicit in opposed trends in 19th century philosophy of science. The philosophy of the naturalist trend is known as positivism. Its early protagonist was Auguste Comte. Comte saw in the emergence of a science of society the last stage in an evolutionary process of liberation of rational thought, first from the tutelage of religion and then from the illusions of metaphysical speculation. Mathematics and astronomy with the Ancients, physics since the Renaissance, chemistry and biology since the Enlightenment had already entered the 'positivist' stage. Now it was the turn of the humanities. The older and more mature members in this ancestral tree set the pattern for the younger members. Thus mathematics for physics, physics for the other natural sciences, and the natural sciences for the social sciences. For the last Comte also uses the name *physique sociale*. The uniform line of descent is a warrant of the Unity of Science. It is illuminating to compare Comte as the philosophic herald of a new science of man with Bacon as a herald of a new science of nature. Neither one of the two visionaries made a contribution to the actual progress of science. Comte's understanding of history and society is as poor compared to Marx's as is Bacon's understanding of physics compared to Galileo's. Both Comte and Bacon were imbued with belief in the usefulness of science as an instrument of human progress. Comte's famous characterization of the aim of science as *savoir pour prevoir pour pouvoir* is the technological spirit in a nutshell. When applied to natural science it

means man's mastery of nature. When applied to the humanities it does *not*, however, mean anything which could reasonably be called man's mastery of himself. Comte's slogan rather suggests a use of scientific knowledge about men for purposes of manipulating human beings for various ends and goals. Whose ends and goals – and manipulation by whom? These questions have obvious answers when we deal with a technology based on natural science. For the social technology based on knowledge of human beings they constitute a grave and open problem.

8. I do not think one can answer these questions without also challenging the philosophy of science which made it urgent to raise them. The challenge was actually made towards the end of the last century in the form of a reaction against positivism. The reaction aimed at defending the autonomy of the humanities in relation to the natural sciences. Various efforts were made to capture the essential differences between the two types of inquiry and in particular to tell wherein the peculiar character of the humanities consisted. Windelband described the difference with the terms *nomothetic* and *ideographic*: in the study of nature we look for generalities and laws, in the study of man and human creations we are interested in the individual and unique. Dilthey exploited the difference between explanation and understanding (*Erklären* and *Verstehen*). The natural sciences explain phenomena by subsuming them under laws; in the *Geisteswissenschaften* we try to understand their meaning and significance.

This early hermeneutic or interpretative philosophy of the humanities was, however, an episode rather than the beginning of an era in the history of thought. Soon positivism made its return – this time equipped with the powerful methodological tools of modern mathematical or symbolic logic. In its heyday between the two wars, logical positivism thought that it had swept the philosophic stage clear of metaphysical rubbish once and for all and laid the foundation of a *wissenschaftliche Weltauffassung*. The enthusiasm was soon tempered, but a lasting impact of the new positivism came to prevail in the diverse currents and trends which can be subsumed under the elastic label of 'analytical philosophy'. Heterogeneous as this phenomenon is, it is still possible to speak of a characteristic climate of opinion in philosophy, ultimately inspired by the positivism of the Vienna Circle and by what used to be called the Cambridge School of Analysis. This climate prevails in the English-speaking countries and in Scandinavia and is making headway, it seems, also on the European continent. In this tradition great contributions have been made to logic and the study of the foundations of mathematics, and to the methodology and philosophy of the natural and other 'exact' sciences. But I should say without hesitation that the contributions to the philosophy of the humanities have been remarkably poor. This fact reflects, I think, a *Zeitgeist* which is uncongenial to humanistic thought and study.

9. The failure of behaviourism, positivism, logical empiricism, and other 'naturalistic' trends in the philosophy of science to provide a satisfactory philosophic basis for the humanities is, in my opinion, due to something I should call *conceptual poverty*. The phenomena which the humanities study have features of their own which distinguish them logically from the typical objects of study in the natural sciences. A primary task of a philosophy of the humanities is to try to capture and do justice to those features. It goes without saying that I cannot accomplish this task in the second half of a brief paper. To think otherwise would be naive and preposterous. The task can perhaps be completed only through a long process of change and maturation in an intellectual climate of opinion. What I can do here is only to indicate a direction in which I think we should proceed in the search for a more adequate philosophy of the humanities than any which has so far been suggested.

10. I characterized the humanities as the study of man as a being of culture. This suggests that the phenomena which the human sciences study are, somehow, 'cultural'. What this means, however, can be understood only if we first pay attention to another, more basic, feature of human phenomena. This is their *intentionality*.

Saying that intentionality is a characteristic of phenomena connected with human culture is, roughly, saying that those phenomena have a *meaning*. A special case of this is linguistic meaning. Another is when the meaning is something aimed at or pursued through the phenomenon in question. In the first case, the bearer of meaning is a 'text', i.e. a document of language. In the second case it is either the action of some individuals or groups or a practice or an institution of society. These two types of meaning, moreover, are closely interwoven. The subject matter of a text is often intentional phenomena. Indeed, without the records which texts provide, a major part of humanistic study would be strictly impossible. Mankind would then have no *recorded* history. But more than this: All forms of human life which can be called instituted and the perpetuation of which is called, in a wide sense, 'tradition' depend on the fact that man is a speaking creature. Were not man a being of language, he would not be a being of culture either – and he would literally have no *history* different in character from that of any other zoological species.

However, we must not exaggerate the uniqueness of man's position in the animal kingdom. Intentional, meaning-carrying phenomena are not exclusively human. Nor are they necessarily language-dependent. It is not anthropomorphism to attribute to a dog fear of punishment consequent upon some mischief. But it would be anthropomorphism to attribute to it remorse at having snatched a piece of meat from the butcher's shop. This is so because remorse is a much more developed form of intentional reaction than fear – and probably one which is inconceivable without language and interpersonal relations under rule.

The recognition that intentionality and language are characteristically even if not exclusively human will help us see, why the conceptual frame of physics, chemistry, or biology is not sufficient for an account of human phenomena in their fullness. In order to understand man as a being of culture concepts are needed which simply have no *application* to, say, mice and rats, not to speak of inanimate objects. Therefore it is a mistake to think that the concepts which suffice for describing and explaining physico-chemical reactions or even sub-human forms of animal behaviour could, either by themselves or as a reduction basis for complex logical constructions, exhaust the conceptual store of the humanities.

To make this statement is, of course, not to prove it true. A philosopher of a positivist orientation would probably also agree that intentionality is a characteristic of everything connected with human culture. But he would deny that intentional phenomena are irreducible to non-intentional ones. In defense of his view he might, for example, put forward a behaviourist theory of meaning.

11. Intentional phenomena have to be *understood* and, when this is connected with difficulties, *interpreted*. Understanding their meaning or significance precedes any attempt to explain their existence or origin; this is one difference between intentional and non-intentional phenomena. It is therefore not inappropriate to call the humanities *hermeneutic* or *interpretative* disciplines.

Calling the humanities hermeneutic and saying that meaning is a characteristic of the phenomena which they study is also to touch on a grave philosophic problem. What is meaning? This question has been very much at the centre of 20th century philosophy. No one could dispute, I think, that the philosopher whose thoughts in the area were most influential and most original was Wittgenstein. He had no clear and simple answer to offer. But from what he has said about intentionality, language, and meaning useful hints can be got also for that which was *not* Wittgenstein's immediate concern, viz. a philosophy of the humanities.

A basic thought of Wittgenstein's is that a 'private language' is impossible. Language is essentially a 'social affair'. The same holds true also of extra-lingual meaning – at least on the human level.

Saying that meaning is a social affair has two important implications. The first is that meaning is something which is handed down, 'tradited', within a community and therefore has to be learnt and taught. The second is that meaning is intimately connected with action. To learn a first language is not to be given a catalogue of names of objects and perhaps some rules of correct speech. It is to grow up to take part in the life of a community, to learn 'how to do things with words': calling persons, asking for objects and for help, reacting to commands and warnings, answering questions – at a later stage also describing things and events and speaking about what is not immediately at hand in space and time. In order to understand the meaning of actions and words, one must therefore either be another member of the same community or otherwise become familiar with, i.e. learn to participate in its 'culture' or ways of life.

12. Both understanding *what* intentional phenomena mean and explaining *why* they occur makes reference to rules. Just as we cannot understand speech without mastering the rules of linguistic practice, we cannot grasp the significance of or the reasons for most human actions without knowing the conventions and regulations, say, for greeting people, honouring the dead, driving and parking cars, getting commodities against payment, transacting one's daily business in the role of official, employer or employee, teacher or student, child or parent, etc., etc. Also most human wants and needs – with the partial exception of those which we share with other species of the animal kingdom – get articulated in the set frame of societal rules and institutionalized patterns of behaviour.

One can make a useful distinction between rules which define a practice and rules which prescribe what ought to or may or must not be done, between constitutive rules and regulative rules, as one sometimes calls them. Then one can give a summary characterization of the way rules relate to explanation and understanding of behaviour by saying that constitutive rules make us understand the meaning of actions – e.g. how bowing to a person can be a way of greeting him – and that regulative or prescriptive rules explain why actions are done – e.g. that I stopped my car because the red light appeared.

13. I shall now advance a thesis which I am sure many will find controversial but which I think is true and, moreover, crucial for understanding the methodological status of the humanities and the relation of the humanities to the sciences of nature. The thesis goes as follows:

Just as natural, i.e. non-intentional phenomena are 'governed' by natural laws, i.e. principles which tell us either what will invariably or in statistical average be the case under in principle recurrent and repeatable circumstances, in an analogous manner intentional phenomena are 'governed' by normative rules which tell us what people under given circumstances are (or were) expected or allowed or practically necessitated to do. I am, in other words, pleading for what might be called a 'methodological parallelism' between natural laws on the one hand and laws and other societal rules on the other hand. I am inviting you to see the difference between the humanities and the natural sciences in the light of the difference between the factual and the normative, between rules which state how things in fact go and rules which ordain how they should go according to the conceptions of those who instituted the rules.

14. It might be objected that what I have said holds true at most only for those humanistic disciplines which are in a strict sense historical. Undeniably the normative web which gives a meaning to the actions of individuals and regulates life in society sets the frame of reference for any account of human affairs we call 'history' – from naive chronicle and narration to the most ambitious attempts at understanding the significance of events and explaining their connections.

Consider narration. An account which limits itself to telling 'wie es gewesen' in the most straightforward sense of this debateable slogan will primarily be about the individual and collective actions of men: how they built and organized their communities, how they cultivated the land, how they traded, waged wars, worshipped and observed various ceremonies – also of the decisions and heroic deeds of great individuals at momentous stages in the peoples' lives. Even if such a story is being told quite naively in the sense that it does not aim at explaining anything, it would not be intelligible unless it described the agents' actions in terms of the institutionalized behaviour-patterns which alone give the actions a 'meaning'.

History, however, is not only chronicle, it is also 'explanation'. We want to know why the actors on history's stage performed as they did – how their actions were motivated by their personal aims or by their duties in assigned roles as kings or governors or priests or judges, say. We also want to estimate the significance of their actions to later developments, i.e. to see how what they did – for whatever reasons – in its turn became a factor in the motivational background for the actions of other people. We can call such explanation 'causal' if we wish. But 'causal' does not then mean 'nomothetic'. The historian does not unravel laws which made events inevitable. He interprets what took place as adequate responses within given institutional frames to the aims and ends towards which human action was directed. Sometimes what happened will appear inevitable in retrospect – as a practical necessity under the circumstances, but not as a causal or natural necessity under the impact of a universal law.

15. Someone who agrees to this may yet argue that it only shows how different history proper is from the non-historical study of man as a being of culture in the social sciences or in linguistics and philology. Do not the non-historical humanities aim at the discovery of law-like regularities of various forms of human behaviour: economic, political, religious, etc., in much the same way as the natural sciences investigate law-like regularities among natural phenomena? Maybe it is vain to look for universal laws in history, but surely there are laws of economics, for example. This we need not deny. But I would maintain that the situation with regard to laws in economics is not as like the situation in, say, physics as some wish to think and not as unlike the situation in historical research as it may appear. Also in the overtly non-historical study of human phenomena there is implicit an essential element of historicity. Not to have recognized this is, I think, a valid criticism which can be levelled against much of contemporary research in the social sciences. I shall try to illustrate what I mean with a very simple example.

Suppose someone wanted to explain the fact that all silver coins vanished from circulation and only paper money remained in the market during, say, the temporary occupation of country *X* by power *Y* in an armed conflict, by reference to what is known as Gresham's law. To say that coins ceased to circulate because there is a law to the effect that, when two kinds of money of unequal exchange value are available for payments, the one of inferior value tends to drive the one of higher value out of circulation – to quote the standard formulation – sounds to my 'logical ear' like a joke and I hope that you, upon consideration, will share my feeling. Compare this with the following case:

Suppose we explain – to paraphrase a famous example – the bursting of a waterpipe during a frosty night by reference to the law that water expands when it freezes. If one is curious one can ask *why* water expands when it freezes. But whether or not this question is raised and can be answered, one will understand why the pipe burst – and if one is incredulous one can make experiments and watch the result. One need only accept the law as fact in order to admit that it has explanatory force.

It is different with Gresham's law. It has no explanatory power *of its own*. Unless we understand *why* 'bad' money should tend to drive 'good' money out of circulation, mere reference to the fact that it does does not make what happened a whit more intelligible. To understand why 'bad' money drives 'good' money out of circulation is easy enough, however, but to understand why water should expand when it freezes is not at all easy. If people fear that the paper money issued by the occupants will be declared valueless once the occupation is over, whereas silver coins at least retain their metal value, then it is clear that people are reluctant to give away what they have in silver and maybe even anxious to buy up coins in exchange for paper money at a nominal over-value. This is a thoroughly understandable motivational mechanism. We have seen impressive examples of its working. To have drawn attention to this is a merit for which Gresham deserves to be remembered. But even if nobody had ever thought of this as a 'law' of economic behaviour, we could readily have explained in an individual case why 'bad' money drove 'good' money out of circulation. What is required is only familiarity with the institution of money and the idea of a market – and, one could add, with 'human nature', i.e. the needs and wants of normal men in a society which knows these institutions.

In order for so-called laws of economic, political, and other forms of social behaviour to have explanatory force, we must first understand *why* they are valid, i.e. we must know the institutional frame within which behaviour in accordance with the law is an adequate intentional response to the challenge of a given situation. Therefore, when the institutional frame changes, previously valid laws may loose their applicability to otherwise similar situations. Thus, for example, it has often been noted that the laws of 'classical' market economy cannot be expected to hold good for the strongly 'manipulated' market characteristic of late capitalist societies, nor for rigidly planned socialist economies.

In this difference in the nature and role of 'laws' one of the *deep* differences between the natural and the human sciences manifests itself. And for reasons connected with this I would claim that the so-called non-historical behavioural sciences are not really 'non-historical'. Theorizing about economic and other forms of social behaviour means devising conceptual schemas which can be used for the analysis and interpretation of phenomena in given historical situations – such as, for example, present-day Western industrialized society. The use of theory in the human as well as in the natural sciences is for explaining and making us better understand the world in which we live. But since the world men build for themselves, i.e. social reality, changes as they go on building it, its explanatory principles – and not only our knowledge of them – will change too in the course of this process.

16. I shall conclude with a return to the question which arose with Renaissance humanism concerning man's place in the world-order. We are now in a position to assign both to Pico the humanist and to Kepler the scientist a due share in the truth. But the greater share belongs, I think, to Pico.

By saying that man has a place in the world-order we could mean that human actions and institutions can be explained in terms which are extraneous to the individual agents and to the institutions in question themselves. Maybe some human phenomena have a spontaneity which defies explanation; and the same may hold true for some natural phenomena. But by and large this is *not* the case – neither in nature nor even with man. Events in nature have causes and what men do and achieve has reasons in terms of which we understand and explain them. To this extent we may say that Kepler was right against Pico.

But in a most important sense we can also say that man's place in the world-order is not *fixed*, if by 'fixed' we mean determined by factors which are extraneous to human action. There are, of course, biological aspects of human life, which makes man's position in this sense fixed too: environmental conditions of temperature, composition of the atmosphere, possibilities of nutrition, etc. But the phenomena specific to man as a being of culture are different. The factors in the terms of which we interpret and explain those phenomena are the creation of man himself: the level of knowledge and technology, the educational institutions, the force of custom and tradition, the normative fabric of the legal order. Once these factors are 'instituted', their determining influence on individual action may extend to minute details of life and even seem like 'iron necessities'. But it would be a fatalistic misunderstanding not to realize that they are man-made and therefore subject to change effected by man himself.

The destiny of men therefore is not written in the stars – neither in the literal sense Kepler had in mind and we regard as superstitious, nor in the extended sense which alone makes Kepler's idea worth taking seriously, viz. that the achievements of men are the predetermined results of forces over which man has no control. If one calls the place of man in the order of things 'fixed' at all, one should remember that the one who fixed it was man himself – though by no means always those men whose actions now are guided and whose freedom is restricted by the rules of the 'fixers'. The possibility is always open that men will refuse the order under which they live and re-fix their place in the world.

NOTE

[1] For the comparison and contrast Pico-Kepler I am much indebted to the excellent introduction by Rolf Lindborg to his translation into Swedish of Pico's 'Oration'. Lindborg, Rolf, *Giovanni Pico della Mirandola Om människans värdighet*, Publications of the New Society of Letters at Lund 71, Lund 1974.

W. V. QUINE

GRAMMAR, TRUTH, AND LOGIC

It is a general practice, in intellectual pursuits, to argue from the truth of one sentence to the truth of another. Some such arguments are the business of logic, others not. They belong to logic if they hinge purely on the structure of the sentences concerned, rather than depending on content. But the structure of sentences consists in grammatical constructions. Here, then, is the intimate connection between grammar, truth, and logic. Logic studies the truth conditions that hinge solely on grammatical constructions.

By this account, to say that one sentence logically implies another is to say that the two sentences are so related, in respect of grammatical form, that no two sentences so related are respectively true and false. The definition becomes more manageable if we break it down into a sequence of three definitions. First we define a grammatical form as *logically valid* if all sentences of that form are true. Next we define a sentence as *logically true* if it has a logically valid grammatical form. Finally we say that one sentence *logically implies* another if the conditional sentence, formed of these sentences in that order by applying 'if' to the one and 'then' to the other, is logically true.

Logical implication is the central business of logic. Logical truth would be of little concern to us on its own account, but it is important as an avenue to implication. It is simpler to theorize about truth than implication because it is attributable to single sentences whereas implication relates sentences in pairs.

I have said that a logically true sentence is a sentence having *a* logically valid grammatical form. For it will commonly have several other grammtical forms as well. The sentence 'If it rained then it rained or it snowed' is logically true by virtue of being of the logically valid for 'If *p* then *p* or *q*', but it is also of the grammatical forms 'If *p* then *r* or *q*' and 'If *p* then *s*', neither of which is logically valid.

But we have still to say what counts as a grammatical form. The sentence:

(1) If sugar is sweet then something is sweet

S. Kanger and S. Öhman (eds.), Philosophy and Grammar, 17–28.

is one that we should like to call logically true, on the grounds that the form:

(2) If x is F then something is F

is logically valid. But is this a *grammatical* form? Certainly 'If x is F then salt is F' would not be a purely grammatical form; the word 'salt' does not qualify as a mere grammatical particle. Why does the word 'something' so qualify? How can we tell what morphemes to count as full-fledged lexical elements and what ones to regard as mere particles marking grammatical constructions?

There is a quite natural criterion of a quantitative kind. Thus consider the particle 'and'. What other morphemes could be substituted for 'and' in all sentences without producing ungrammatical strings? Very few: 'or', 'but', and little else. Or again consider the suffix '-ed'; surely there is no other that could be substituted for it in sentences without usually engendering nonsense. Such is the cramped nature of grammatical particles. For a lexical element, on the other hand, there are no end of substitutes that preserve grammaticality. If for almost any common noun in a sentence you substitute almost any other common noun or noun phrase, the result may be false and may be bizarre, but it will be grammatical. Similar fluidity prevails in the various sorts of verbs and adjectives and in the singular terms. The morphemes in all these categories belong to the lexicon. Such, then, is the quantitative criterion: a morpheme is a particle or a lexical element according as there are few or many expressions in its grammatical category.

The word 'something' does seem more substantial than a grammatical particle. It is substantial and even substantival; it occurs as subject and object of verbs. By our quantitative criterion, however, it is still a grammatical particle. It does not belong to a large grammatical category of substantives. 'Something' can be supplanted by 'salt' in some sentences without producing ungrammatical results, but there are other sentences in which such substitution produces incoherence – such a one as 'There was something new on the Rialto'. Substitution gives 'There was salt new on the Rialto', and this must presumably be disqualified, not just as an absurd sentiment, but as flatly ungrammatical. Such cases suffice to dissociate 'something' from 'salt' in respect of grammatical category.

The word 'something' actually has little company in its grammatical category. It has the word 'nothing' for company, perhaps, and a few others. Thus it is that 'something' qualifies as a grammatical particle by our criterion, and accordingly (2) qualifies as a grammatical form by our criterion, and so (1) qualifies as logically true by our criterion.

Actually this example can still be contested in another way. It may be objected that 'something' is not a morpheme but a noun phrase consisting of two morphemes. This is reasonable, but it does not affect our conclusion; for the morpheme 'some' still qualifies as a logical particle, and so does 'thing'. This is established still by the example 'There was something new on the Rialto'; neither 'some' nor 'thing' admits of many substitutes in this context without incoherence. So (2) still qualifies as a logical form, and (1) as logically true.

I suppose the first example one thinks of in the way of a logical particle is 'not'; so we would surely want this to turn out to be a grammatical particle by our criterion. We may start to worry, then, when we reflect that 'not' can be supplanted in most contexts by countless adverbs without incoherence. However, the situation is again saved by a few quirks of idiom. It is saved by the context 'not only'.

Granted, I am treading rather rocky terrain. Cases of what we would like to regard as logical truth might still turn up that are not saved by any quirk of idiom, and cases of what we would not like to regard as logical truth may issue from quirks of idiom. The firm boundary will depend rather on some actual tampering with grammar on the logician's part. I shall come to that presently.

Meanwhile let us remind ourselves of another point: in drawing lines between grammatical categories we are dependent still on a distinction between the merely absurd sentiment and the flatly ungrammatical; for we had to rule that 'There was salt new on the Rialto' is ungrammatical. Carnap's example, 'This stone is thinking about Vienna', would be viewed as absurd but grammatical; so also, probably, would Russell's example 'Quadruplicity drinks procrastination'. What is required as a wedge between grammatical categories is not just the absurd, but the ungrammatical. How do we draw that line? William Haas has offered an interesting answer.[1] An appropriate occasion for the merely absurd can be built up in a fanciful fairy story. The more absurd the example, the more difficult the build-up; it is a matter of degree. But the ungrammatical cannot be accommodated at all in stories, however fanciful; it can be accommodated only by concocting deviant dialects.

Thus far we have laid up two logical truths: 'If it rained then it rained or it snowed' and 'If sugar is sweet then something is sweet'. We are apt to run thus to conditionals, since each logically true conditional presents an implication, and implication is the object of the game. Now here, according to the definition, are two more for our growing collection:

> If Tom is taller than Dick then Dick is not taller than Tom.
> If Tom is taller than Dick and Dick is taller than Harry then Tom is taller than Harry.

The grammatical particles concerned here are 'is', 'not', 'then', 'and', and the suffix '-er'. There can be no quarrel with these logical truths or the corresponding implications, but they are not in the logic books. Let us see why. What they reflect is the asymmetry and transitivity of two-place predicates formed with the suffix '-er'; and the point is theoretically insignificant, because many other predicates share those same properties without flaunting them with any marker such as '-er'. This is as it should be, since the asymmetry or transitivity of some predicates may even be an as yet undiscovered fact of nature. Moreover, asymmetry and transitivity are merely two among endlessly many properties of various predicates; why single them out? The natural course is just to state them as premises where needed.

Are we to say then that our proposed definition of logical truth and implications is faulty after all, and that 'Tom is taller than Dick' does not really imply 'Dick is not taller than Tom' logically? And correspondingly for the transitivity example? No, I would adhere to the definitions. I think most people would agree that these examples are good logical implications, even though they are not in the books. I say that they are not in the logician's book because the logician is revising grammar itself, and that the definitions of logical truth and implication in terms of grammar continue to be good. Revision of grammar is an important part of the logician's activity, and I want to discuss its nature and purposes.

His revision of grammar in the present instance does not change the boundary between grammatical and ungrammatical expressions. Some of his other revisions do, as we shall see; but this one is only a change in the way we analyze the expressions. When he skips the asymmetry and transitivity of 'taller than' as none of his business, we may think of him as repudiating the grammatical particles '-er' and 'than' and treating 'taller than' as a single morpheme. It is an attractive move semantically, by the way, since 'tall' makes no clear sense anyway except by comparison. A tall man is tall for a man but not for a building; and 'tall for a man' simply means '*taller than* most men'.

Relative to grammar as thus revised, the asymmetry and transitivity of 'taller than' cease to count as logical implication; for they are not reflected in the new grammatical structure. But they may continue to be recognized as implication in a broader, extra-logical sense. Implication in this broader sense holds in many cases where there is no suggestion of relevant grammatical structure. An example is the symmetry of 'cousin': 'Tom is Dick's cousin' implies, in some sense, 'Dick is Tom's cousin'. Such implication rests on meanings of lexical elements, not on grammatical particles; and what is vague about it is the notion of meaning. Now the asymmetry and transitivity of 'taller than' continue to qualify as implications in this vaguer semantic sense, even if with the revisionary logician we view 'taller than' as a monolithic morpheme.

For the latter-day logician, logical regimentation of grammar is standard procedure. We have noted the motivation of one such reform, and it is characteristic of many. Others of his reforms serve to resolve structural ambiguities; others serve to economize on constructions. His interest in grammatical structure is onesided: he is interested in how it channels truth conditions. If a grammatical reform makes for a more copious channeling of truth conditions and causes no complications in other quarters, he is happy to adopt it. He adopts it not as a reform to be imposed on society, but as a technical by-language to expedite scientific inference. The shift is the same in principle as programming a computer, and the same, for that matter, as the mathematician's habitual recourse to planned notations.

Would it be trivial to argue merely that the logician *can find* a revision of grammar that would make the grammatical forms coincide with the logical forms intuitively so-called? No, this would not be trivial; not if the revised grammar was still adequate to an all-purpose scientific language. But anyway what I mean to say goes beyond this: I am talking of the logician's motive. He is not revising grammar merely to fit grammatical form to what he already happened to call logical form. My thought is rather this: what we call logical form is what grammatical form becomes when grammar is revised so as to make for efficient general methods of exploring the interdependence of sentences in respect of their truth values.

Let us therefore consider, from a practical point of view, what line the logician's grammatical regimentations might have been expected to take. Let us proceed as if we did not know the line actually taken. We may caricature him as a consulting technician whose job it is, given two sentences of some science, to determine whether the one implies the other. He will unite them in a conditional and regiment its outermost structure first. He will then work inward as needed, stopping when he has established logical truth. His first concern will thus be with grammatical constructions that are capable of being outermost – hence with sentence-forming constructions. His is a strategy of shallow analysis: expose no more structure than is needed for the purpose at hand. In paraphrasing the constructions of ordinary language into his regimented grammar, moreover, he will cheerfully relinquish various connotations of the old idioms, unless they seem germane to the scientific business in hand. He will be intent on truth conditions, since he is seeking logical truth. Taking these considerations together, we may well expect the logician's first concern to be with sentence-forming constructions, and of these we may expect him to favor truth functions where he can.

The necessity operator, like the truth functions, builds sentences from sentences. Some logicians admit this construction to their regimented grammar. Others, however, exclude the notion – not just from logic, but altogether – as obscure and ill-conceived. There are further constructions, of course, that likewise build sentences from sentences. One is 'because'. This construction cannot be so lightly dismissed from general discourse as the necessity idiom can, but it is equally problematic. The causal relation is notoriously obscure, obscure out of all proportion to what it would contribute to logical truth or implication. Further constructions that build sentences from sentences are the idioms of propositional attitude – thus '*x* believes that *p*', '*x* hopes that *p*'. These again are not to be lightly dismissed from general discourse, but they are logically inert: patterns of implication are not in evidence at all, except that '*x* knows that *p*' and '*x* regrets that *p*' and a few others may be said to imply '*p*'.

The truth functions, at any rate, emerge as the logician's first concern. But he cannot rest thus with the resolving of sentences into component sentences. There are implications that depend on more fragmentary components. Here again, heeding the maxim of shallow analysis, the logician will shun undue fragmentation.

What a sentence says about anything can be assembled in a self-contained expression by means of a grammatical construction that I call *predicate abstraction*. It is the 'such that' construction, and is a logical regimentation of the relative clause. The role of the relative pronoun is played by a bound variable, and the words 'such that' are rendered by an inverted epsilon. Thus consider the sentence 'Paul lost his passport'.

What it says about Paul is '$x \ni$ (x lost x's passport)'. What it says about his passport is '$y \ni$ (Paul lost y)'. These 'such that' clauses are not names of properties or classes; they are mere predicates, tantamount to relative clauses or to verb phrases. The clause '$x \ni$ (x lost x's passport)' is equivalent to the predicate 'lost one's passport', and the clause '$y \ni$ (Paul lost y)' is equivalent to 'lost by Paul'. The point of converting to the 'such that' style, with its variable, is that is extracts or abstracts predicates uniformly from all manner of sentences, without requiring various structural transformations within the sentence. To get the predicate 'lost one's passport' in the vernacular we had to change an original 'his' to 'one's'; to get the predicate 'lost by Paul' we had to switch to passive voice; and other examples would call for other maneuvers, often quite devious. The 'such that' construction well illustrates what the logician is up to in his grammatical reforms. He seeks structural uniformity so that his tests or proofs of implication may proceed smoothly according to general rules.

Observe, moreover, the contrast between this modification of grammar and the earlier reform that consisted in treating comparative adjectives as single morphemes. That was only a change in the mode of analysis, and did not affect the linguistic output. On the other hand the 'such that' construction comes as an innovation even in outward form.

Predication is the grammatical construction that consists in adjoining a predicate to a singular term to recover a sentence, thus:

[$x \ni$ (x lost x's passport)] Paul,
[$y \ni$ (Paul lost y)] (Paul's passport).

Each of these sentences collapses to 'Paul lost Paul's passport' by the logical law of *concretion*.

Predicates are not only for predicating. If that were their only use, there would be no point in predicate abstraction. Instead of predicating '$x \ni$ (x lost x's passport)' of Paul or other persons, we could as well write Paul's name or others in place of 'x' in 'x lost x's passport'. Another conspicuous use of predicates, however, is in existence statements. The existence functor '$\exists$' attaches to a predicate to form a sentence, true or false according as there is or is not anything that satisfies the predicate. Thus the combination of symbols '$\exists\ x \ni$' amounts in the more usual notation to the quantifier '$(\exists x)$'. Actually the line of evolution that I am describing is not fanciful. The functor '$\exists$ and the prefix '$x \ni$' are lifted verbatim, or literatim, from the pioneer work of Peano, where existential quantification emerged explicitly as that combination.

In practice I do use the notation '(∃x)', but there is some philosophical point in analyzing it as '∃ x ∍'. The predicate abstract, or 'such that' clause, is a direct regimentation of the relative clause, and the use of variables in predicate abstraction is the use that most clearly reflects what bound variables are wanted for. In all their familiar uses – in quantification, in singular description, in class abstraction – their essential contribution is the same: by their recurrences they keep track of permutations and repetitions of references. There is in this nothing distinctive to do with classes or description or the universal and particular categoricals. Where we see the variable clear of foreign entanglements is in the 'such that' clause. Here the variable emerges as an instrument purely of extrication: of rearranging a sentence around some chosen component, so as to segregate it from something it was about. As for quantification, description, and class abstraction, these are most naturally rendered directly as functors upon predicates; any variables present are for abstracting those predicates themselves. We already saw '∃' as a sentence-forming functor on predicates: '∃F', 'there are F'. The 'x' of '(∃x)' gives way to the 'x' of abstraction of the predicate to which '∃' is applied. The '∀' of universal quantification becomes another sentence-forming functor on predicates: '∀F', 'everything is F'. The '℩' of description becomes a term-forming functor on predicates: '℩F', 'the F'. Class abstraction calls for an unaccustomed term-forming functor 'ɔ': ɔF is the class of all Fs. The variable, properly considered, is neutral amid all this. It is simply the heir to the relative pronoun.

It is well known that names and other singular terms can be dispensed with in favor of predicates and bound variables. Instead of inventing a name 'n' to pick out some object uniquely, we could as well invent a predicate 'P' which is to be true of that object uniquely. Then, instead of embedding the name 'n' in a sentence, '. . .n. . .', in order to say something about the object, we could as well embed an existentially quantified variable in the sentence, subject to the identifying predicate 'P'; thus,

$$(\exists x)(Px \cdot \ldots x \ldots), \quad \text{or} \quad \exists\ x \ni (Px \cdot \ldots x \ldots).$$

In practice even in formal logic it is more convenient to keep the names and other singular terms, but their eliminability is instructive in a number of theoretical connections, including the present one.

I characterized predicate abstraction as a way of segregating what a sentence says about an object. Commonly the predicate thus abstracted does not exhaust what the sentence says about the object, since the term that designates it will also say something about it in order to identify it. Now that we have eliminated singular terms other than variables, however, designation goes by the board; there is only the variable. All that an open sentence says about the value of the variable is said by the rest of the sentence; the variable says none of it. The variable is the legitimate latter-day embodiment of the incoherent old idea of a bare particular.

The logician's regimented grammar has come down to something slight. Conjunction and negation suffice as truth functions. In addition there is predicate abstraction, with its variables, and there is '∃'. Or we can lump these latter two together and call it quantification, '∃ *x* ∍'; for the logician needs the two only thus combined. Predication of predicate abstracts was seen to be pointless, so predication is not called for under the logician's regimentation. As for universal quantification, it can be got from existential quantification and negation in familiar fashion; thus '∼∃*x*∍∼'. We have got down to the grammar of standard or neo-classical logic; simply quantification and the truth functions.

Some logicians opt for more. Commonly, of course, they provide a grammatical niche for singular terms other than variables; but this can be seen as a mere matter of style, since it can be avoided without theoretical loss. Some logicians allow also for tense, but this is avoidable by admitting time as values of variables and exploiting temporal predicates such as 'earlier than'. Some logicians admit, as remarked, a modal necessity operator.

I said that the logician's central concern is logical implication, and that the avenue to it is logical truth. For establishing logical truth he needs a formal technique or calculus. It is directed to the recognizing or generating of logically valid grammatical forms; for the forms, not the sentences, are what present the bare logical essentials. The sentences differ from the forms precisely in containing also the filler that does *not* contribute to validity or logical truth, but only gets in the logician's way.

These grammatical forms are depicted notationally in schemata, which depict the grammatical forms of sentences that have been regimented from the outside inward to varying depths. Unanalyzed interior portions of sentences, however complex, are schematized simply by single letters '*p*', '*q*', etc., or by '*Fx*', '*Fy*', '*Gxy*', etc. if we want to signal the presence of variables buried inside them.

Was I wrong, then, in saying that the logician's way of regimenting grammar does not assume predication? Is '*Fx*' not a case of predication? Confusion over this point is almost unavoidable. Quantification logic is even called the predicate calculus, and the schematic letter '*F*' is called a predicate letter. It is quite reasonably called a predicate letter, occupying as it does a position appropriate to a predicate; and the juxtaposition '*Fx*' then does indeed represent predication. But the point to appreciate is that '*Fx*' is no part of the logician's regimentation of grammar. It does not enter the sentences, but appears only on the logician's work sheet. Think of the logician again as the consultant, auditing the scientist's sentences for implication. He paraphrases the outward structure of sentences, imposing his quantifiers and truth function signs. He presses inward, imposing still only quantification and truth functions. When he stops doing that, he just abbreviates the unanalyzed internal residues as '*p*' or '*q*' or '*Fx*' or the like; the '*Fx*' says nothing about grammatical structure, but merely reminds him that there is a free occurrence of '*x*' somewhere inside.

I have been eliciting the logician's regimentation of grammar by reflecting on his concern with truth links and his strategy of paraphrasing inward. Because of his maxim of shallow analysis, he is not called upon to inquire into the atomic structure of sentences. Once he has paraphrased deep enough to clinch a desired implication, he will render any as yet unanalyzed segment of text by a schematic letter or so – no matter how complex that segment may be. The structure deeper in the interior is not his concern.

An easy further step, however, produces a self-sufficient grammar: we may take simple predicates, with one or more variables attached, as the atomic sentences. The logical grammar then suffices to generate the superstructure. Such is the blueprint for a general scientific language. In such a language the grammatical form of any sentence is precisely its logical form, plus predication at the atomic level: predication of one-place simple predicates and of many-place ones as well. Such predication is an additional grammatical construction, for we saw that predication had no place in the grammatical structure that the logician imposes in paraphrasing inward from outside. In recognizing predication thus at the atomic level we round out a self-contained grammar, but we add nothing to the logical truths or implications. The grammatical structure that we have projected into the atomic sentences proves to be logically inert.

It will be recalled that the predicate abstraction that was the mainstay of our logical grammar produced only one-place predicates. Only in our present little excursion into the atomic level are we recognizing many-place predicates, and we are finding them logically inert. This is puzzling, for we were brought up to believe rather that a major strength of modern logic lies precisely in its mastery of many-place predicates. We have been told that the formal logic of past centuries was inadequate to the logic of relations and that it was the glory of modern logic to have overcome this limitation.

We can clear up this puzzle by considering what that old limitation was, more exactly, and how it was overcome. Described anachronistically in terms of variables, the limitation was that no two variables could occupy an unanalyzed part of a sentence. Thus picture the old-fashioned logician paraphrasing the outward structure of a sentence and working inward. His analysis will never reach the point of exposing two references to objects, unless it exposes them as occupying opposite components of some already exposed grammatical construction; this was the old limitation. When we recognize the 'such that' construction as a part of logical grammar, we overcome that limitation. Analysis can proceed to the point of exposing a predicate within a predicate, e.g. in the manner:

$$x \ni \exists y \ni (\ldots x \ldots y \ldots),$$

and there it can quite well stop, leaving the unanalyzed interior text '$\ldots x \ldots y \ldots$' with the two variables associated no matter how. Thus it is that the abstraction of one-place predicates, when nested, can do many-place business.

We saw how to extend the logician's regimented grammar into atomic sentences to form an overall grammar for a language. It is perhaps rash to say that a language with that grammar can be generally adequate. We may well dismiss the necessity operator as useless or unacceptable, but one hesitates to be so cavalier with the idioms of propositional attitude. Still I do see this language pattern as a valid ideal of clarity. I find a scientific theory finally satisfactory only if I can see how to cast it in such a form.

In closing I should say something of the logic of identity, which I have persisted in skirting. I have been characterizing logical truth and implication by grammatical structure. This account excludes the logic of identity, since the identity sign is no mere grammatical particle but a predicate in the lexicon. The exclusion seems odd, since we always think of identity theory as part of logic.

We can recognize logic in a narrow sense as hinging wholly on grammatical structure, and so as excluding the theory of identity, and logic in a somewhat wider sense as hinging on grammatical structure and the identity predicate. This latter concession is not altogether arbitrary. A notable trait of logic is its central position in our conceptual scheme; it is an integral part, as Tarski has remarked, of every branch of science. Now identity is similarly central. It is definable, nearly enough, in each particular language, so long at any rate as the lexicon of simple predicates is closed off at some finite point. For, as is well known, we can then define '$x = y$' by exhaustion of atomic contexts:

$$Fx \equiv Fy \cdot \ldots \cdot (z)(Gxz \equiv Gyz) \cdot (z)(Gzx \equiv Gzy) \cdot \ldots .$$

If we view identity as so defined, there is a way after all of admitting identity to logic without giving up our grammatical theory of logical truth. We can view the identity sign as a schematic predicate symbol, subject to a different interpretation in each particular language. The languages concerned are all to share the regimented grammar of truth functions, quantification, and atomic predication that we have been contemplating. They differ from one another only in their lexica of simple predicates. The identity sign, then, becomes a schematic symbol which is to be interpreted in each of these particular languages by exhaustion of the atomic contexts in that language. True sentences of the theory of identity then – '$(x)(x = x)$', '$(x)(y)(x = y \cdot \supset \cdot y = x)$', and the like – become logical truths after all, in the strict sense of being logically valid grammatical forms, when interpreted according to that plan in each particular language. On this plan the identity sign does not qualify as a grammatical particle, but its laws still belong to logic.

NOTE

[1] 'Meanings and Rules', Proceedings of the Aristotelian Society, 1973, pp. 135–155.

DAGFINN FØLLESDAL

COMMENTS ON QUINE

This symposium is a meeting-ground for three disciplines that by and large have stayed together from their beginning and are today interacting as actively as ever:

linguistics, philosophy, and logic.

During this symposium we have heard papers that have taken up themes that are of common concern to these three disciplines. The paper we have just heard is, however, the only one which in its very title brings together all three disciplines, with one key word from each:

grammar, truth, and logic.

The papers presents briefly Professor Quine's views on what the relationship is between these three disciplines, expressed succinctly in one brief sentence in his book *Philosophy of Logic*:

'Logic chases truth up the tree of grammar.'[1]

The paper we have heard is a description of this chase.

I shall now comment on some points in the paper which, it seems to me, would be well worth discussing by our group. I will concentrate on the following three points:

1. Logical particles.
2. Syntactic ambiguities.
3. Demonstratives.

1. LOGICAL PARTICLES

One hundred and fifty years ago, Bolzano[2] was the first to have the idea of demarcating logic the way Quine does with the help of a set of logical particles which are held constant, while the other non-logical expressions are freely substituted for one another. However, Bolzano's idea received little attention until it was rediscovered afresh in the mid-thirties by Quine and Ajdukiewicz[3] independently of one another. All the basic

S. Kanger and S. Öhman (eds.), Philosophy and Grammar, 29–35.

ingredients are there in Bolzano: the steps that Bolzano goes through are the same as Quine's and in the same order:

1. Specify a vocabulary of logical particles.
2. Define what it means for two expressions to have the same logical form:

> Two expressions have the same logical form if they can be obtained from one another by the substitution of non-logical expressions for non-logical expressions.[4]

3. Define logical truth:

> A sentence is logically true if and only if all sentences with the same logical form are true.

As for step 2, Bolzano, like Quine, places two restrictions on the substitutions:

(a) The words that are substituted for one another have to belong to the same substitution class. (The notion of substitution class is only rudimentary in Bolzano, but is worked out by Husserl, to whom Quine gives credit in *Philosophy of Logic*.)

(b) The substitution must be uniform, i.e. when an expression is substituted for another it must be substituted for it in all places where it occurs.

One important restriction that Bolzano is not aware of, but that Quine mentions in his *Philosophy of Logic*,[5] was only hinted at in Quine's paper today. This is that substitutions for pronouns must be such that they do not change the system of cross references that the pronouns are part of. The point of this limitation is easily shown in a regimented language, where one uses variables instead of pronouns. If one treats variables as belonging to the lexicon and also, as is natural, as belonging to the same substitution class, then from

$$\ldots x \ldots y \ldots$$

one would presumably get

$$\ldots x \ldots x \ldots$$

by substitution of '*x*' for '*y*'. However, these two expressions do not have the same logical form, nor are they normally supposed to have thc same grammatical form. Hence complications enter into our hitherto simple approach to logical and grammatical form. We may, for example, introduce restrictions on substitution. This destroys our neat picture, the motivation being semantical: one of the main reasons for defining logical validity by way of logical form is that we want to define validity without bringing in a notion of meaning. Alternatively, we may regard variables as logical or grammatical particles rather than as part of the lexicon. However, there are many of them, and this therefore complicates the picture.

A philosophically much more important difference between Quine's approach and that of Bolzano's is, however, the following which I think is well worth discussing:

While Bolzano held that he could see no principle by which one could distinguish the logical particles from the non-logical expressions[6] – all one could do was to write down a list, but what to include and not to include seemed arbitrary – Quine puts forth such a principle: He suggests that the logical particles are grammatical particles and that these in turn are those expressions in our language which have the *smallest substitution classes*.

Quine has set forth this idea earlier in his *Philosophy of Logic*.[7] It seems strange that the notions of logical form and logical truth should hinge on something so accidental as the size of substitution classes. However, neither in *Philosophy of Logic* nor in this paper does Quine give much by way of argument why this should be so. The main reason he gives is expediency: it simplifies grammar to treat as particles words that do not go into large substitution classes.

There seems to be considerable evidence against there being a correlation between small substitution classes and logical particles. On the one hand, there are clearly non-logical terms that have very small substitution classes. Consider for example the prepositions in German that take the accusative, or even worse, the two prepositions 'längs' and 'zufolge' that take either the dative or the genitive. Similarly in the Scandinavian languages many prepositions have very small substitution classes. In Norwegian, for example, the preposition 'til' in some rare cases takes the genitive, 'til havs', etc.; this is a remnant of an old genitive. It may be acceptable to regard these words as particles in grammar, but certainly not in logic.

On the other hand, and this is more important, there seem to be logical terms that have large substitution classes. Identity, i.e. '=', is a case in point; its substitution class apparently includes most terms for binary relations. However, Quine in his paper has shown how to get rid of identity as a particle. The variables are another case. As we remember, one way of avoiding restrictions on substitution was to treat the variables as logical particles. If we do this, then clearly we have a group of logical particles that belong to a very large substitution class.

In view of these difficulties, let us ask ourselves: Which words can be expected to have small substitution classes? Here are three kinds of such words:

(1) Words that are frequently used and therefore become incorporated in particular idioms.

(2) Words that are used in many fields and accordingly many kinds of linguistic neighborhoods.

(3) Words that are remnants of old grammatical constructions.

Now, (1) and (2) are likely to comprise the logical particles, since the logical particles are used often and in connection with all kinds of subject matter, in all cases where language is used. Words of type 3, however, do not seem to have any particular tie to logic.

These, then, seem to me to be the main reasons why there is some affinity, but no complete correspondence, between logical particles and small substitution classes. In a regimented language, of course, words of type 3 will be likely to be eliminated; they do not help simplify the chase of truth. Note in this connection that our chase of truth will perhaps yield different logics depending on the peculiarities of the language from which we start. We have at present no reason to expect the resulting logic to be unique.

2. SYNTACTIC AMBIGUITIES

According to Quine, grammar should generate all and only the well-formed strings, with some rounding-off. There is a remarkable parallel between this enterprise and the task of building up a system of ethical princples, along the lines of Rawls.[8] We start out from a set of basic intuitions concerning individual cases. These institutions are more or less firm from case to case. We then try to formulate some general principles that fit in with all these intuitions. However, these principles influence and change some of our intuitions, particularly the less firm ones. Given these revised intuitions, we have to go back to our principles again in order to revise and simplify them. Thus we go back and forth until, hopefully, we reach what Rawls has called a 'reflective equilibrium'.

However, in addition to generating the right strings, a grammar is normally expected to account for syntactic ambiguities. How can this be done without a notion of difference and sameness of meaning? It seems that we cannot simply construct the best grammar that fits in with all our intuitions concerning meaningfulness and expect that this grammar will yield two or more different derivations for all and only those sentences which, upon reflection, we regard as syntactically ambiguous. We have been given no reason to expect that the notion of syntactic ambiguity can be extracted from the notion of meaningfulness in this way. In the absence of such reasons, we should regard our intuitions concerning syntactic ambiguity as equally fundamental to our grammar as our intuitions concerning meaninglessness.

This position is further confirmed by the fact that, as we saw earlier, the distinction between difference and sameness of meaning also seems called for in connection with the restrictions on substitution of variables. In dealing with variables Quine seems faced with a dilemma: either he may treat the variables as logical particles, but then he has to give up the view that the logical particles have small substitution classes; or else he may treat the variables as part of the lexicon, but then he needs restrictions on substitution that are motivated semantically by considerations concerning whether sentences have the same or different meanings.

3. DEMONSTRATIVES

The way Quine conceives of the logician's regimented grammar, names and other singular terms are dispensed with in favor of predicates and bound variables. Instead of using a name – to pick out some object uniquely, one uses a predicate, simple or composite, which is true of that object uniquely.

However, there is, I think, a demonstrative element in names that is not captured when reference is channeled through predication. A genuine referring expression, as opposed to a definite description as commonly used, aims at getting at some particular object and sticking with it regardless of how the object changes and regardless of the various mistaken beliefs we may have concerning the object. When our theories change, preservation of reference is generally more important than preservation of extensions for the predicates. This idea of genuinely referring expressions is what Donnellan, Kripke, Kaplan, Putnam, and others have tried to capture through their theories of reference and demonstratives. Quine sees in the variable "the legitimate latter-day embodiment of the incoherent old idea of a bare particular". This old idea of a bare particular, incoherent as it often was, was, I think, an attempt to deal with the phenomenon of reference, and I agree with Quine that the variable is a prime example of a genuinely referring expression. However, there are clearly others as well, in particular most proper names.

Many of our uses of referring expressions are accompanied by ostension, e.g. pointing. In trying to understand somebody and translate what he says, ostension is an important part of our evidence. This evidence is not taken into account when we regard all singular terms other than variables as disguised definite descriptions. If we model reference on descriptions, we come to hold that a name refers to whatever object happens to satisfy the associated definite description uniquely, if there is such an object. What we should do instead is the following: Consider a case where, according to our way of understanding what a person does and what he says, we take one of his movements to be an attempt to indicate a reference by pointing. We should then assume that what he refers to is one of the objects in the direction in which he is pointing or an object related to one of these through what Quine calls 'deferred ostension'. We should do this even if the predications he makes should fit some other object better. In a satisfactory theory of interpretation and translation, therefore, the evidence that we gather by ostension should override considerations based on maximizing agreement.

This, then, appears to be a decisive flaw in the attempt to channel all references through predication.

NOTES

[1] Quine, W. V., *Philosophy of Logic* (Prentice-Hall, Englewood Cliffs, N.J., 1970), p. 35.

[2] Bolzano, Bernard, *Wissenschaftslehre* I–IV (J.E. v. Seidelsche Buchhandlung, Sulzbach, 1837).

[3] Quine, W. V., 'Truth by Convention', in O. H. Lee (ed.), *Philosophical Essays for A. N. Whitehead*(Longmans, New York, 1936). Reprinted in W. V. Quine, *The Ways of Paradox* (Random House, New York, 1966), and in various other places, including Herbert Feigl and Wilfrid Sellars (eds.), *Reading in Philosophical Analysis* Appleton-Century-Crofts, New York, 1949). Ajdukiewicz, Kazimierz, 'Sprache und Sinn', *Erkenntnis* **4** (1934), 100–138.

[4] It makes a difference here whether by 'non-logical expression' we mean 'expression which is not a logical particle' or 'expression which neither is nor contains a logical particle'. In the latter case, once the vocabulary of logical particles has been fixed, the logical form of an expression is determined uniquely, i.e. each expression belongs to just one class of equiform

expressions. In the former case, an expression may be said to instantiate several different logical forms, depending on which of the logical particles in the expression are kept constant and which are included in the expressions that are permitted to vary. This pluralistic notion is what Quine makes use of when he says that a logically true sentence is a sentence having *a* logically valid form. Also, the pluralistic notion is useful in connection with Quine's *maxim of shallow analysis*: in checking the validity of an argument, expose no more structure than needed. (Quine in this paper and in *Word and Object*, (MIT Press, Cambridge, Mass., 1960, p. 160.))

[5] Quine, *Philosophy of Logic*, second printing, p. 59. Quine's remarks were prompted by Gilbert Harman's review of the book in *Metaphilosophy* **2** (1971), 184–190.

[6] Bolzano, *Wissenschaftslehre*, Section 148, Part 3 (=Vol. II, p. 84).

[7] Quine, *Philosophy of Logic*, p. 29.

[8] Rawls, John, *A Theory of Justice* (Harvard University Press, Cambridge, Mass., and Oxford University Press, Oxford, 1971).

JAAKKO HINTIKKA

THEORIES OF TRUTH AND LEARNABLE LANGUAGES

By far the most interesting and most successful recent theories of meaning have been truth-conditional. The paradigm of such theories is usually taken to be Tarski's recursive characterization of truth for certain formal languages.[1] Donald Davidson has both practiced truth-conditional theorizing in the semantics of natural languages and pleaded for the general importance of truth-conditional semantics.[2] What is even more interesting and more unique to him, Davidson has sought to give a deeper motivation – perhaps a foundation – for truth-conditional semantics of the kind pioneered by Tarski. This deeper foundation Davidson has sought in the requirement of *learnability* of the language in question.[3]

An attempt to link semantics and language learning to each other is not completely new. For instance, Wittgenstein used to illustrate his semantical claims by reference to how certain parts of language are learned or could be learned. Furthermore, highly interesting work has recently been done in mathematical linguistics on the precise formal conditions of learnability for various explicitly defined languages.[4] However, Davidson seems to be unique is using learning-theoretical ideas to support a Tarski-type approach to the semantics of natural languages. He does not claim that the learnability of a language implies the existence of a Tarskian truth-theory for it, but he clearly thinks that this is the most natural form of truth-theory for a learnable language. Even if learnability does not necessitate the availability of a truth-characterization, it makes such a characterization eminently natural, Davidson thinks.[5] In the form of a slogan, theories of meaning for learnable languages are supposed to become so many theories of truth for these languages.

The mediating link between learnability and a recursive truth-theory is what Davidson calls the *Frege Principle*, that is to say, the principle which says that the meaning of a complex expression is a function of the meanings of its constituent parts.[6] Since we are dealing with truth-conditional theories of meaning, we can in this paper equally well consider the corresponding referential principle which says that the extension (reference) of a complex expression is a function of the

S. Kanger and S. Öhman (eds.), Philosophy and Grammar, 37–57.

extensions (references) of its constituent parts. Linguists know the Frege Principle as the principle of *compositionality*.[7] Learnability is supposed to bring us close to the Frege Principle, and the Frege Principle is expected to make feasible a Tarski-type truth-definition.

I disagree sharply with this overall conception of Davidson's. Accordingly, what I shall argue in this paper is the following. First, I shall suggest that learnability alone does not make compositionality very natural. Secondly, I shall argue in terms of a list of examples that compositionality fails in natural languages in a wide variety of ways. Thirdly, a number of supplementary issues of a partly historical character are discussed. They lead by stages to an overall evaluation of Davidson's approach to linguistic semantics. Fourthly and finally, I shall briefly suggest that what the learnability requirement principally motivates is a theory of truth different from Tarski's and independent of the requirement of compositionality. As you can see from this summary, I am not rejecting the idea of truth-conditional semantics, even though I believe that philosophers and linguists usually think of such semantics in seriously oversimplified terms.

Why should the learnability of a language make us expect that the Frege Principle holds for it? Davidson does not present an explicit argument but something along the following lines is what he seems to have in mind.[8]

Learnability presupposes that the meaning of a given complex expression, say E, can be gathered from a finite number of clues in E. Moreover, these clues have to be syntactical, based either on the vocabulary of E or else on the structure (structural features) of E. In either case the meaning of E can be said to be recoverable from its several constituent features or components. In this sense, the meaning of E is a function of the contributions of its several constituent components or parts.[9] But such a contribution of a constituent part e to the meaning of the larger whole can safely be identified with its meaning, the meaning of e – or so it seems.[10] (After all, the meaning of any expression is supposed to be its use in language.) Hence the meaning of the whole is determined by the meanings of its components, that is, the Frege Principle is valid.

The crucial step in this train of thought is the identification of the meaning of a component part e with its contribution to the meaning of the larger complex expressions E in which e can occur. This amounts to a reification of use into meaning. Its fashionability notwithstanding, this hypostatization needs a closer scrutiny. It is largely to safeguard this step, it seems to me, that Frege introduced the other principle frequently associated with him. This is the principle according to which a word or other simple grammatical constituent has meaning only in a context.[11] As Wittgenstein later put it: "Only propositions have sense; only in the context of a proposition does a name have a meaning" (*Tractatus* 3.3). It should be clear why it was in effect resorted to by Frege here. If a constituent part *e* could have a meaning also in isolation, there would not be any general guarantee that its meaning in the context of a complex expression *E* should be identical with its meaning in isolation. Then the contribution of *e* to the meaning of *E* could not be identified with the meaning (meaning *simpliciter* or meaning in isolation) of *e*, and the argument just sketched would be fallacious. Frege attempted to escape this problem by denying that it can arise.

A brief historical comment may be in order here. Frege admittedly never considers (as far as I know) his second principle as a response to a challenge directed against his first principle (compositionality). However, a closer examination of what he in fact does serves to vindicate my way of explaining Frege's procedure. It is seen for instance from the beginning of § 62 of *Grundlagen* what the second Frege principle was supposed to do. It was calculated to enable Frege to say that any contribution to the meaning of a sentence by a word can be considered as the meaning of that word (in the sense that this contribution of the word is what its definition specifies). This freedom would be severely limited if we could assign to the word some fixed reified meaning already in isolation. This is what Frege is doing in the passage referred to. Hence the motive I have ascribed to Frege is a special case of his real motivation. Accordingly, I am not violating the spirit of what Frege is doing here.

Frege's attempted way out is inadequate, however. What is at issue in the difficulty just mentioned is much more general than a possible difference between meaning in isolation and meaning in context. The real, general problem is that the meaning of *e* might vary, even when it is thought of as the contribution by *e* to the meaning of a complex expression *E* in which *e* occurs. Imbed *e* in a different context *E*′, a critic might aver, and its role in determining the meaning of the whole will be different. Then there would not be any such thing as *the* contribution of *e* to the respective meanings of the different complex expressions in which *e* can occur, and the hypostatization employed in our experimental argument cannot succeed. The second Frege principle deals with this problem only in the special case in which the second context *E*′ is the empty one, *e* occurring in splendid isolation. Even if the principle were correct, it would therefore solve only a small part of the real problem.

Simply *saying*, as Frege in effect does, that we can always identify the contribution of a component expression to the thought expressed by the sentence in which it occurs with its meaning (sense) does not make it possible. We can still ask whether the contribution is the same in different contexts. The general principle Frege is relying on here would for instance enable him to say that 'is' has a unique sense, viz. its contribution to the different thoughts it can help to express, even though Frege himself treats on other grounds 'is' as being ambiguous.

Hence we can see a serious flaw in Davidson's argument, or, rather, in the argument sketched here as a possible rational reconstruction of his line of thought. Learnability alone does not suffice to motivate the Frege Principle. It is only in conjunction with another assumption that learnability can serve to motivate compositionality. This further assumption is a kind of context-independence of meaning. The meaning of an expression must not depend on the context in which it occurs. For the purposes of the present paper, I shall call this assumption the *context-independence thesis*. If this thesis does not hold, we face the problem just indicated, and the role of *e* in determining the respective meaning of the complex expressions in which it can occur cannot be reified into any one entity with which the meaning of *e* itself could be identified.

The assumption of context-independence is closely related with another thesis, and can even be considered as a variant of the latter. This new thesis says that the proper direction of semantical analysis is from inside out in a sentence or other complex expression. I shall call this the *inside-out principle*.[12] Its connection with the context-independence principle is clear. If the meaning of *e* depends on the context $E(e)$ in which it occurs, the meaning of $E(e)$ cannot be analyzed from inside out. For if we tried to do so, we would run into an impasse: the meaning of *e* could not be decided on the basis of its 'inside', for by assumption it depends on the context, i.e., on what there is 'outside' it. Hence we could not process it semantically by proceeding always from the inside out.

Another assumption among the interrelated principles we have to consider here is the one which asserts that syntactical and semantical rules operate in tandem. I shall call it the *parallelism thesis*.[13] To each syntactical rule of formation, telling us how a complex expression *E* is constructed from simpler ones, say $e_1, e_2, \ldots, e_i$, there corresponds according to the parallelism thesis a semantical rule which tells how the meaning of E depends on the meanings of those of the simpler input expressions, $e_1, e_2, \ldots, e_i$.

I suspect that the parallelism thesis has been instrumental in encouraging semanticists to believe in the inside out principle. If you accept the parallelism principle and believe that the rules of syntax work from inside out (this is what characterizes all generative grammar), you very easily slip into thinking that the rules of semantical interpretation do the same, i.e., that the inside out principle holds. This would be a mistake, however. The parallelism thesis is distinctly different in its implications from the inside-out principle and from the context-independence thesis. The parallelism thesis implies the inside-out principle only on certain further assumptions. The most important of them is the assumption that when E is formed from certain simpler strings $e_1, r_2 \ldots, e_i$, these very expressions will become *parts* (constituent expressions) of E. Otherwise the dependence of the meaning of E on those of $e_1, e_2, \ldots, e_i$ (prescribed by the parallelism thesis) will not be of the kind the Frege Principle asserts: the meaning of E will admittedly depend on those of $e_1, e_2, \ldots, e_i$, but these will not be constituent parts of E, for they may be changed when E is built up out of them. We shall call the assumption that forces $e_1, e_2, \ldots, e_i$ to be actual parts (constituent components) of E the *invariance thesis*.

The invariance principle can be said to hold in virtually all formal languages. It also holds of many of the simpler syntactical generation rules for natural languages. It is for instance related rather closely to what is known among grammarians as the cyclic principle. This principle deals with the case where $e_1, e_2, \ldots, e_i$ are clauses (subordinate sentences) and E a higher sentence. There is no general *a priori* reason, however, why the invariance thesis should be valid.

In envisaging possible failures of the invariance thesis even when the parallelism thesis holds, we are not dealing with a mere abstract possibility, either, but with a kind of behavior which is exemplified by what happens in an actual semantical theory. In my game-theoretical semantics the meaning of a complex expression E is typically analyzed in terms of the meanings of certain simpler expressions $E_1, E_2, \ldots, E_j$.[14] These simpler expressions are obtained from E through certain game rules, and their syntactical relation to E is determined so closely that we can (at least for the sake of the present argument) think of E as being constructed from $E_1, E_2, \ldots, E_j$. Nonetheless, they are not always themselves *parts* (constituent components) of E in any natural sense of the word. Hence, game-theoretical semantics can be said to violate the invariance thesis, even though it can be hoped to preserve a form of parallelism between syntax and semantics.

Another additional assumption necessary for the purpose of obtaining the inside out principle from the parallelism thesis is that the meaning of E must be *completely determined* by the meanings of the expressions E_1, $E_2, \ldots, E_j$ from which it is constructed. For otherwise the meaning of E is not a function of the latter. It is far from clear that this stronger thesis holds of all the formation rules of fairly simple formal languages. A striking counter-example to it will nevertheless be found later in this paper; see the type (v) counter-examples discussed below.

This requirement will be called the *determinacy thesis*.

If learnability alone implies any of the assumptions we have discussed, it implies the parallelism thesis. This thesis seems to come fairly close to Davidson's purpose when he says that the meaning of each sentence can be established on formal grounds alone.[15] For this reason, it is of interest to see that parallelism does not *ipso facto* imply the Frege Principle without substantial additional assumptions.

The main dependencies among the assumptions I have most recently examined can be summed up in the following schema.

$$\text{learnability} \rightarrow \left.\begin{array}{l}\text{parallelism}\\ \text{invariance}\\ \text{determinacy}\end{array}\right\} \rightarrow \text{compositionality}$$

The dependence of the Frege Principle on the context-independence thesis suggests where to look for counter-examples to compositionality in natural languages. Whenever the meaning (interpretation) of an expression depends on the wider context, a violation of the Frege Principle is in the offing. This heuristic idea has proved most useful in locating counter-examples to compositionality in English, some of which will soon be outlined. These examples will conversely illustrate and otherwise throw light on the context-independence principle. In this respect the examples below which deal with the behavior of 'any' and with backwards-looking operators are especially instructive.

Another method of finding counter-examples to compositionality is suggested by the determinacy thesis. It might seem that this thesis is trivially valid. For when E is constructed from $e_1, e_2, \ldots, e_i$, nothing is added to them. They are merely combined or given a structure in a certain way (assuming invariance). And this structure is nothing new (or so it may be alleged). It must be indicated syntactically, and hence it must be represented by one of the constituent features $e_1, e_2, \ldots, e_i$.

This attempted vindication of determinacy fails, however. If the determinacy thesis and the Frege Principle are to have any real bite, a postulation of the 'constituent parts' they speak of (here, the constituent features $e_1, e_2, \ldots, e_i$) must have independent syntactical motivation. They must in some straightforward sense be *syntactical* parts of E. But there are many properties of English sentences which are not indicated by any clear-cut syntactical marks. Some of them will turn out to have important semantical functions, and hence give rise to failures of determinacy. I shall later present examples of such breakdowns of determinacy. The best example is probably the behavior of branching (partly ordered) quantifiers in formal as well as in natural languages. As I have remarked in earlier papers,[16] in natural languages like English informational independence is not usually indicated by any single grammatical feature. Even in formal languages, there is no 'logical constant' to mark informational dependencies and independencies.

Hence we have here a failure of determinacy: whether or not the quantifier phrases of a sentence E are independent is not determined by any number of constituent parts of E.

The following is a survey of some of the most conspicuous failures of compositionality. Of these counter-examples, (*i*)–(*iii*) can be traced to contextual dependence, whereas (*iv*)–(*v*) illustrate the breakdown of determinacy.

(*i*) I have shown earlier that the English quantifier word 'any' interacts with its environment.[17] In a game-theoretical treatment, this is shown by the fact that the game rule (G.any) for 'any' has priority over a number of other rules (even when these other rules apply to expressions in higher clauses or further on the left). These rules include game rules for negation, modal concepts, and 'if'. Accordingly, we can expect to find counter-examples to compositionality in these contexts. This expectation turns out to be justified. It is especially interesting to see that happens in a context which contains intensional concepts over and above negation. The following is a list of examples of the failure of the Frege Principle.

(1) Chris can win any match.
(2) Jean doesn't believe that Chris can win any match.
(3) Chris will beat any opponent.
(4) Chris will not beat any opponent.

(5) Anyone can beat Chris.
(6) I'll be greatly surprised if anyone can beat Chris.
(7) Any businessman can become a millionaire.
(8) The sentence 'Any businessman can become a millionaire' is true if any businessman can become a millionaire.

Of these, (3)–(4) require a comment. It is not clear that (3) can be taken to be a constituent part of (4). Not very much turns on this question. However, how else can you generate a negated sentence except from the corresponding unnegated one?

I shall return to (7)–(8) later.

(*ii*) Another class of linguistic phenomena which exhibit semantical context-dependence are the ones which Esa Saarinen has sought to deal with in terms of his 'backwards-looking operators'[18]. Their nature is best seen from formal systems of modal logic. If we think an of an outside in evaluation procedure being applied to a sentence of such a system, you can easily see that such an evaluation procedure is always a one-way journey. We start from a given world, the one at which the sentence is being evaluated, move to one of its alternatives, then perhaps to an alternative to this alternative, and so on. (The game-theoretical semantics I have developed serves to vindicate this intuitive picture.) However, we can never return to worlds considered earlier. The world of conventional modal logic is like the world of Thomas Wolfe: in it, you can't go back home again.

It nevertheless turns out that several different phenomena in natural languages presuppose a return to worlds considered earlier. The simplest method of treating such phenomena formally is to introduce explicit operators which tell us to return to an earlier world. This is what Esa Saarinen has done in his work on what he calls 'backwards-looking operators'. They are precisely the return ticket operators I mentioned. From my description we can also see that those operators depend on their context. They presuppose a 'memory' as to what happened in evaluating those parts of the sentence which lie farther outside. Hence they violate the inside-out principle and thereby the Frege Principle.

It turns out that natural languages have few, if any, explicitly indicated backwards-looking operators and that the return to earlier worlds therefore has to be accomplished in them by other means. This does not militate against what I just said of there being counter-examples to Frege in natural language, however. What is left open is merely the question concerning their closest formalization.

The following series of examples, adapted from Saarinen ('Backwards-looking Operators', 1977, Note 18 above) illustrates these counter-examples.

(9) A child was born who would become ruler of the world.

(10) Joseph said that a child had been born who would become ruler of the world.

(11) Balthazar mentioned that Joseph said that a child had been born who would become ruler of the world.

Each of these has more ambiguities than its predecessor. The moment of the child's becoming the ruler of the world is in (9) in the future as looked upon from the moment of birth; in (10) it can also be in Joseph's future; and in (11) it can even be in Balthazar's future. In other words, the semantical interpretation of the innermost clause varies with its context.

(*iii*) Probably the most illuminating way of viewing backwards-looking operators is to consider them as allowing anaphoric back reference to worlds considered earlier in the same evaluation process. Since the world in question is usually specified by expressions outside the context in which the backwards-looking operator in question occurs, the operator introduces a violation of the thesis of context-independence and hence a violation of the Frege Principle.

Similar things can obviously be said of several other kinds of expressions with an anaphoric function. Their semantical evaluation depends on taking into account ('remembering') a wider context considered earlier in the evaluation process, sometimes because the head phrase occurs in that wider context and sometimes because the anaphoric expression is for other reasons context-dependent.

This suggests a direction in which further counter-examples to the Frege Principle can be expected to be found. This expectation turns out to be justified. However, it also turns out that really striking counter-examples are not generated as much by the ordinary anaphora leading us out of a given context as by context-dependencies of other kinds. In particular, the purely anaphoric uses of the definite article do not give rise to as clear-cut counter-examples as those uses (which we shall not otherwise discuss here) where 'the *X*' operates as it should on Russell's theory of definite descriptions provided that quantifiers are restricted to individuals mentioned earlier in the evaluation ('introduced earlier in the semantical game').[19] In other words, 'the *X*' refers à la Russell to the one and only X among the ones which the semantical game has so far produced. The context-dependence of this semantics of 'the' is obvious. The following example shows how it leads to a violation of the Frege Principle.

(12) Even the best mathematician sometimes makes mistakes.

(13) Thomas, Richard, and Harold were classmates in school. Thomas was the best mathematician, Richard the best cricketeer, and Harold the most amusing story-teller.

(*iv*) A phenomenon of an apparently different kind is the behavior of quantifier scopes in English.[20] Not only is it the case that quantifier scopes are not marked in English; they are in a very real sense not determined in English. Or, they extend arbitrarily far not only in one and the same sentence but also in discourse involving many sentences. You can begin a sentence by saying something about 'an old man' and keep on referring to 'him' or 'the old man' all through the sentence and all through shorter or longer bits of discourse, perhaps throughout an entire book (if you are Ernest Hemingway).

This indefinitely large scope of natural-language quantifiers alone shows or at least strongly suggests that the Frege Principle cannot possibly hold in natural languages like English. For what are the component parts of an English sentence containing quantifiers? Whatever they are, one requirement is clear: whenever such a part contains a quantifier, it must include all of the scope of that quantifier. But if this scope extends arbitrarily far, there cannot be any such parts at all. The Frege Principle is thus shown to be false or at least inapplicable.

When we try to convert this observation into a specific counter-example to compositionality, however, we face a technical problem. This problem is that the wide scopes of some natural-language quantifiers are as it were merely potential. In order to actualize them, we need pronouns or other vehicles of anaphoric cross-reference. It is in such references back to a quantifier that the scope of the quantifier can be seen. Moreover, we can hope to obtain an obvious counter-example only when the back reference changes the semantical status of the original quantifier. Otherwise we can still in each particular case hope to analyze the situation in keeping with compositionality by including enough of the sentence (or discourse) in the scope of the quantifier. Hence the specific examples one can find here will depend on some other semantical phenomenon over and above the indeterminacy of quantifier scopes.

The following examples can be thought of as exemplifying these remarks.

(14) Bills owns a donkey.
(15) If Bills owns a donkey, he beats it.

In (15) the context somehow changes the existential quantifier 'a' into a universal one. The mechanism of the change is explained by Carlson and Hintikka elsewhere.[21] Suffice it to say here that the explanation shows that the semantical interpretation of the consequent of (15) depends on what happens in the antecedent. This context-dependence is the reason why the Frege Principle fails in (15).

Even though the phenomenon of indefinite quantifier scopes is relatively hard to cash in in the form of particular examples (for reasons explained above), it is one of the most characteristic features of natural languages. It involves a clear violation of the spirit of the Frege Principle.

(*v*) It is interesting to see that the Frege Principle can fail even in some formal languages. There are two main types of such failures. Both are dealt with most naturally in game-theoretical terms, and have in fact been so treated by logicians independently of my game-theoretical semantics.

(a) In one, an outside-in game can go on to infinity. The best known case is what logicians call languages with game quantifiers.[22] They cannot be dealt with by means of Tarski-type recursive truth-definitions because such a definition must start from atomic propositions and work its way up to complex ones, while infinitely deep languages are characterized precisely by the sometime absence of such absolute starting-points. In contrast to this failure of recursive truth-definitions, there is no difficulty in treating such 'bottomless' languages game theoretically. The only novelty that is needed is a definition for winning and loosing for certain infinitely long games. But they do not present any insuperable difficulties to a game theorist.

Among languages of this sort there are, besides the well-known game quantifier languages, also the languages defined in Hintikka and Rantala (1976).[23]

(b) The kind of logical behavior exhibited by these infinitary languages is not found in natural languages, with the possible partial exception of certain semantical paradoxes. There is another interesting mode of logical behavior, however, which is much closer to what happens in natural languages. It is the behavior of partially ordered (e.g., branching) but otherwise normal first-order quantifiers.[24] As is shown in detail by Jon

Barwise,[25] such quantifiers violate the principle of compositionality. They can easily be dealt with game-theorctically, however, In particular, the intuitive reason why they are not subject to the Frege Principle allows a simple explanation in terms of game-theoretical semantics. What makes quantifiers branch instead of being linearly ordered is the fact that the game choices associated with a given quantifier may depend on the choices associated with only *some* of the outer quantifiers (quantifiers within the scope of which the given one apparently occurs), not on *all* of them. (The quantifiers it depends on are the ones occurring earlier in the same branch.) This is a clear violation of the inside-out principle, for it means that the interpretation of a quantifier depends on its relation to 'outside' quantifiers (quantifiers occurring outside its own scope.) Small wonder, therefore, that branching quantifiers violate the Frege Principle.

Even if partly ordered quantifiers occurred only in formal languages, they would constitute a forceful reminder of the limitations of Tarski-type truth-definitions aimed at by Davidson. They are made an even more telling counter-example to the Frege Principle by their presence in natural languages. I have argued this point at length in earlier papers, and answered critics.[26] By this time, the main point – their occurrence in natural languages – seems to have been established beyond reasonable doubt. The next two sample sentences (17)–(18) are modest examples to illustrate the role of branching quantifiers in English. They both instantiate the following branching quantifier structure which does not reduce back to the linear form.

(16) $$\begin{matrix}(x)\,(\exists y)\\(z)\,(\exists u)\end{matrix} > M(x, y, z, u)\,.$$

(17) Every villager has a friend and every townsman has a cousin who are enemies.

(18) Some novel by every writer is mentioned in some essay by every critic.

The most persuasive natural-language examples of branching quantifiers probably deal with so-called 'non-standard' quantifier words ('many', 'few', 'most', etc.), as distinguished from logicians' 'standard' quantifiers (the existential and the universal one). It has been claimed by Jackendoff (among others)[27] that sentences containing such words frequently have readings which cannot be explained in terms of quantifier ordering. These readings, allegedly inexplicable in logical terms, turn out to be precisely branching-quantifier readings. The following is a simple case in point.

(19) Few men accomplish as much as many women.

This has been a moderately liberated reading ('there are not many men each of whom single-handedly accomplishes as much as many women'), a feminist reading ('there are not many men who accomplish as much as each of a large number of women'), and a rampant male chauvinist reading ('a small group of men accomplishes as much as many women together'). The first two readings can be obtained by the two possible linear orderings of the two quantifiers 'few' and 'many'. The last reading, however, cannot be so obtained. But it obviously results from making the two quantifiers independent (parallel or 'branching'). The possibility of such a reading in ordinary English shows the presence of branching quantifiers in natural languages.

Indeed, simple branching quantifier structures are more often irreducible in the case of 'nonstandard' than in the case of 'standard' quantifiers. Nonstandard quantifiers are studied by Lauri Carlson in a forthcoming paper. He shows that irreducibly branching quantifier structures are most easily created by branching occurrences of the quantifier word 'few'. (See also Jon Barwise's recent paper on branching quantifiers in English, Note 25 above.)

(*vi*) I have argued on an earlier occasion that the behavior of multiple and iterated questions in English cannot be explained in a satisfactory way without assuming that our tacit methods of semantically processing such questions work from the outside inwards.[28] This involves a violation of the inside out principle and hence a violation of the Frege Principle. The argument is too long to be summarized here. Basically, the problem is to explain why multiple questions have the precise multiplicity of readings they in fact have in English.

What is impressive about these counter-examples to the Frege Principle is that they span many of the most pervasive and most interesting semantical phenomena: quantifier scopes, both relative and absolute; definite descriptions (the definite article); some types of anaphora; multiple questions; generic uses of the indefinite article; and so on. In view of these examples no one can any longer claim that violations of the Frege Principle are marginal or otherwise unimportant phenomena.

It might be thought that one main reason why many philosophers of language believe in the Frege Principle is that they believe in extensionality. There is a historical connection between the two problems in that Frege's formulation of his principle was prompted by his struggles with nonextensional contexts.[29] I don't know if Davidson's distrust of modalities and possible-worlds semantics is connected with his adherence to the Frege Principle.[30] Doesn't the mutual substitutivity of two component expressions e_1 and e_2 occurring in E on the basis of the identity of their references show that the reference of E is determined by those of its parts and that the Frege Principle is therefore valid? No, it does not, for the substitutivity guarantees neither that the semantical contributions of e_1 and e_2 are context-independent (independent of their environment in E) nor that the contributions of such syntactically well-defined parts are collectively sufficient to determine the meaning (reference) of E. This is in fact illustrated by my earlier examples, several of which pertain to first-order languages in which extensionality holds. For instance, the introduction of branching quantifiers does not destroy extensionality, but it does destroy the Frege Principle.

Conversely, some suitable version of the Frege Principle can very well hold in nonextensional contexts. This question is connected with the historical question: Was Frege a Fregean? In other words, did Frege believe in compositionality? Even though he apparently adhered to the principle, some philosophers are in these days assuming as a matter of course that Frege's treatment of oblique (opaque, nonextensional) contexts violated the principle of compositionality.[31] It is quite clear, however, that Frege did not think so. In general, in asking whether the meanings of the component parts $e_1, e_2, \ldots, e_i$ of a complex expression E determine the meaning of E we have to decide whether we are considering the meanings $e_1, e_2, \ldots, e_i$ have *in E* or whether we are speaking of the meanings they would have *in isolation*. Accordingly, we obtain two different versions of the Frege Principle. Can we make the real Frege Principle stand out? As we say, Frege denied that we can really speak of the meanings $e_1, e_2, \ldots, e_i$ would have in isolation. Hence he must have rejected the second alternative. But if we opt for the first alternative, as Frege did, Frege turns out to be a Fregean after all. For on Frege's analysis of opaque contexts the subordinate expression occurring in such contexts refer to what is normally their sense or *Sinn*. In other respects, the reference of the whole is determined as usual. Hence the reference of the whole depends in a regular way on the references *in that context* of its component expressions, which means that the Frege Principle holds in its most Fregean form.

This analysis can in a sense be vindicated in possible-worlds semantics.[32] There the semantical entity associated with, say, a singular term *s* as its meaning or sense is a function from possible worlds to individuals. These meaning functions correspond in possible-worlds analysis to Frege's notion of 'sense'. What happens in, say, a context where we are speaking of John's beliefs is that these functions are restricted to worlds compatible with John's beliefs. Now the alternativeness relation associated with John and with the notion of belief (this alternativeness relation is the appropriate semantical entity determined by the word 'believes') suffices to pick out that class of all possible worlds admitted of by what John believes. (They are the worlds bearing this relation to the given one.) Hence the semantical interpretation of a complex expression is determined by the semantical entities associated with its component parts.

However, other versions of the Frege Principle fail to be satisfied by Gottlob's own treatment. Frege himself in effect admits that the reference of an opaque expression is not a function of what the meanings of its parts would be in isolation. What is even more important, the inside out principle is not satisfied by Frege's treatment by opaque (nonextensional) contexts, even though it can be thought of as being satisfied by the possible-worlds treatment of the same contexts (as long as no backwards-looking operators are present).

The two forms of the Frege Principle therefore differ in their relation to the inside out principle. The one Frege himself appears to have embraced does not presuppose the inside out principle, whereas the other form does. These two forms have not been distinguished sufficiently sharply in recent discussion.

Furthermore, tables can be turned on Frege here. Frege denied that we can speak of the meanings of component expressions, say e_1, e_2, . . ., e_i, *in isolation* from the context (say E) in which they occur. It is not clear, however, that we can always speak of their meaning *within* that *context*, either. In order to see that, we can consider what might happen when the invariance principle fails, as it fails in game-theoretical semantics. Then the meaning of E might be determined by the meanings of certain other expressions e_1', e_2', . . ., e_j', obtainable from e_1, e_2, . . ., e_i and E. Then the procedure for determining the meaning of E might turn completely on the meanings of e_1', e_2', . . ., e_j' and hence bypass e_1, e_2, . . ., e_i altogether. In such circumstances it might be nonsense to speak of the respective meanings of e_1, e_2, . . ., e_i *in the context* E. Again, this is precisely what happens in game-theoretical semantics.

By the way, this is an additional reason why Frege's attempted way out from possible failures of context-independence is inadequate.

But how does Davidson fare amidst all these failures of compositionality? Not very well, it seems to me. He has consistently used as one of his tools in semantics the famous T-schema of Tarski's.[33] In other words, he has required that all the substitution-instances of the following schema be true.[34]

(T) ⌜'*p*'⌝ is true if and only if *p*

where ⌜'*p*'⌝ can also be replaced by a structural description of the same substitution-value of '*p*'.

One of the guiding lights of Davidson's semantics is the requirement that any satisfactory theory of meaning must imply as theorems all the substitution-instances of the schema (T). This way of imposing truth-conditionality on one's semantics is not very happy, however. As I have pointed out earlier,[35] one half of (T) sometimes fails to be true, as witnessed by examples like (8) above. (The other half is in this case ungrammatical, which is also bad for Davidson's purposes.) Now we can see the deeper reasons for the failure of the schema (T). Its failure is merely one example among many of the failures of compositionality. It is not the most straightforward example, but the role of (T) in Davidson's overall research strategy makes it especially dramatic.

Attempts to defuse this criticism of Davidsonic attempts to apply (T) to natural languages have totally failed, it seems to me. For instance, James C. Klagge[36] imagines that he can escape the trouble by in effect replacing (8) by

(20) It is not the case that any businessman can become a millionaire or 'Any businessman can become a millionaire' is true.

But of course (20) says precisely the same in English as (8).

Klagge tries to cheat by inviting the reader to insert 'just' in front of 'any' in (20). This would amount to lending 'any' an emphatic stress, and would therefore change the situation completely here and everywhere else, as illustrated e.g., by the haughty debutante's line, 'I don't dance with *any* boy'. (She could equally well have said, 'I don't dance with just any boy.') It is well known that emphatic stress changes scope conventions in general. Hence Klagge's attempted way out here is without any force.

Klagge's other attempted ways out involve mixing logical symbols and English in the substitution-instances of the T-schema. The truth-conditions of such sentences are not fixed either by logic or by the semantics of English, and are hence useless for elucidating the meanings of English sentences. After all, it was the unproblematic pre-theoretical truth of its substitution-instances that was supposed to make the use of the T-schema so useful.

Notice that there are further problems about the applications of the schema (T) to an ordinary language like English. An instance of the schema is grammatical if and only if the following conjunction is grammatical.

(21) ⌜'*p*'⌝ is true if *p*, and ⌜'*p*'⌝ is true only if *p*.

Earlier, I registered certain difficulties about the first conjunct. There are problems about the second conjunct too. Strings of the form

(22) ⌜'*p*'⌝ is true only if *p*

are typically ungrammatical (unacceptable) if ⌜*p*⌝ contains the word 'any', for reasons I have spelled out elsewhere.[37] Hence (21) is in the same circumstances ungrammatical, too. Thus both halves of the T-schema can fail in English: the one can be false, the other ungrammatical. It turns out that the underlying reason for both is one and the same, viz. the context-dependence of the semantics of 'any'.

Alex Blum's attempted rejoinder[38] to my criticism is equally beside the point. He proposes to modify (T) by allowing '*p*' to be replaced by the interpretation in the canonical notation (of a meta-language) of the sentence whose quote or structural description replaces ⌜'*p*'⌝. This course would not solve the problems I am concerned with but merely push them around. Instead of being problems about the T-schema, they now become problems of translating the critical sentences into one's canonical notation. It is not news that T-schema works in a suitable canonical notation, for instance in a formalized first-order language. But the problem of translating natural language into a quantificational notation is a much more formidable one than philosophers currently seem to realize. Even when they manage to translate some particular sentences, their paraphrases almost invariably remain, in Merrill B. Hintikka's apt phrase, 'miraculous translations': they do not have any real grasp of the general principles or rules their translation relies on.

Indeed, Davidson has made it clear that he considers the use of T-schema a way of avoiding the problem of miraculous translation and relying on our pre-theoretical understanding of a familiar language as a stepping-stone to a semantical theory. This purpose would be completely destroyed if applications of T-schema themselves rely on immaculate translation, as they will do on Blum's suggestion.

Thus by restoring the validity of T-schema Blum is destroying its usefulness for the very purpose it is calculated by Davidson to serve.

Much more important than the failure of any one particular argument or device of Davidson's is the overwhelmingly clear fact that the aims of his whole program are too narrow. The failures of compositionality mean in plain English that there is a large number of sentences in natural languages like English for which no Tarski-type recursive characterization of truth will work. Nor can this failure be blamed on the fuzziness, ambiguities, or other imperfections of natural language. For, as mentioned earlier, there likewise are highly interesting formal languages for which a Tarski-type truth definition cannot work. Hence it seems to me that a radical revision of the whole project is in order.

How is Davidson's program to be revised? I believe that he is right in looking for truth-conditions (and conditions of satisfaction). But we have to take a much longer and harder look at the way those truth-conditions actually operate than anyone, including Davidson, has so far done. Among the features of this actual mode of operation of truth-conditions, it seems to me, there is the fact that they operate from the outside in, which is enough to prove Davidson's aims unrealistic.

How should our truth-conditions operate? If a conjecture is permitted, they should operate in parallel with the processes we actually use in understanding our language. And these processes, it seems to me, are basically anticipations of the operations ('language-games') which link our language with non-linguistic reality. Davidson is indeed right in trying connect truth-conditions and language learning. But what we basically learn are not recursive truth-clauses but the *use* of our language. The time is ripe, it seems to me, to create an entirely new paradigm for truth-conditional semantics.[39]

NOTES

[1] Tarski's classical monograph *Der Wahrheitsbegriff in den formalisierten Sprachen* has appeared in English translation in the volume *Logic, Semantics, Metamathematics* (Clarendon Press, Oxford, 1956), pp. 152–278.

[2] Davidson's most important writings along these lines are the following: 'Theories of

Meaning and Learnable Languages', in *Logic, Methodology, and Philosophy of Science: Proceedings of the 1964 International Congress*, ed. by Y. Bar-Hillel (North-Holland, Amsterdam, 1966), pp. 383–394; 'Truth and Meaning', *Synthese* **17** (1967), 304–323; 'On Saying That', *ibid.*, **19** (1968–69), 130–146; 'True to the Facts', *The Journal of Philosophy* **66** (1969), 748–764; 'Semantics for Natural Languages', in *Linguaggi nella Società e nella Tecnica* (Communita, Milan, 1970), pp. 177–188; 'In Defense of Convention T', in *Truth, Syntax and Modality*, ed. by H. Leblanc (North-Holland, Amsterdam, 1973), pp. 76–86; 'Radical Interpretation', *Dialectica* **27** (1973), 313–328; 'Belief and the Basis of Meaning', in *Mind and Language*, ed. by S. Guttenplan (Clarendon Press, Oxford, 1975); 'Reality Without Reference', *Dialectica* **31** (1977), 247–258.

[3] Cf. for instance the title of Davidson's Jerusalem paper (1966), Note 2 above.

[4] See Peter W. Culicover and Kenneth Wexler, 'Some Syntactical Implications of a Theory of Language Learnability', in *Formal Syntax*, ed. by Peter W. Culicover, Thomas Wasow, and Adrian Akmajian (Academic Press, New York, 1977), pp. 1–60 (with discussion and further references to the literature).

The classical results concerning the non-identifiability of transformational grammars by Stanley Peters and R. W. Ritchie can be understood in the same spirit; see P. Stanley Peters and R. W. Ritchie, 'A Note on the Universal Base Hypothesis', *Journal of Linguistics* **5** (1969), 150–152; 'On the Generative Power of Transformational Grammars', *Information Sciences* **6** (1973), 49–83. It is a pity that Davidson's ideas have never been related to this interesting line of work.

[5] Cf. 'Theories of Meaning', p. 387: 'I do not mean to argue here that is is necessary that we be able to extract a truth definition from an adequate theory [of meaning] (though something much like this is needed), but a theory certainly meets the condition I have in mind if we can extract a truth definition; in particular, no stronger notion of meaning is called for'. Davidson does not discuss the additional assumptions, however, on which we can extract a Tarski-type truth definition from an adequate theory of meaning.

In 'On Saying That' Davidson goes as far as to say that "a satisfactory theory of meaning must, then, give an explicit account of the truth-conditions of every sentence, and this can be done by giving a theory that satisfies Tarski's criteria; *nothing less should count as showing how the meaning of every sentence depends on its structure*" (my italics; p. 131). This is necessary because "by giving such a theory, we demonstrate in a persuasive way that the language, though it consists in an indefinitely large number of sentences, can be comprehended by a being with finite powers". (See *op. cit.*, p. 131.)

The 'Tarski criteria' referred to by Davidson here are not Tarski-type truth conditions, but rather the requirement that one's theory of truth imply all instances of Tarski's T-schema. This schema will be discussed later in my paper.

[6] Cf. Michael Dummett, *Frege: Philosophy of Language* (Duckworth, London, 1973), pp. 152–157, 159–160.

[7] Cf., e.g., Barbara Hall Partee, 'Possible Worlds Semantics and Linguistic Theory', *The Monist* **60** (1977), 302–326, esp. pp. 306–308; 'Montague Grammar and Transformational Grammar', *Linguistic Inquiry* **6** (1975), 203–300.

[8] Even if Davidson should not subscribe to the argument to be presented, it serves to bring out some pertinent aspects of the conceptual situation. The historical accuracy of my 'rational reconstruction' therefore is not a major issue here. Davidson has never spelled out himself in full, explicit detail what the connection between learnability and truth-conditions is supposed to be. Hence every attempt to discuss the rationale of his views is bound to

contain an element of conjecture – or at least extrapolation.

The best way out seems to me to take Davidson literally when he refers to Frege as the originator of the principle and to examine how Frege conceives of it and motivates it.

[9] Cf. Davidson, 'Theories of Meaning', p. 387: ". . . we can regard the meaning of each sentence as a function of a finite number of features of the sentence. . . ."

[10] This identification is made explicitly by Frege, as witnessed by *Grundgesetze* **1**, § 32 (p. 51 of the original, p. 90 of the Furth translation): "The names . . . contribute to the expression of the thought, and this contribution of the individual [component] is its *sense*".

Statements of the same general import are found in Gottlob Frege, *On the Foundations of Geometry and Formal Theories of Arithmetic*, edited and translated by E. H. W. Kluge (Yale University Press, New Haven, 1971), pp. 8, 53, 67.

[11] See Frege, *The Foundations of Arithmetic*, tr. by J. L. Austin, (Blackwell, Oxford, 1950), pp. 71, 73, and cf. Dummett, *Frege* (Note 6 above), pp. 192–196.

[12] Often, the Frege Principle is simply identified with the inside out principle. Later in this paper we shall see that such a terminology would be historically inaccurate, however.

[13] The main function of the compositionality principle (Frege Principle) is often seen in effecting this parallelism between syntax and semantics. Cf. e.g., Partee, 'Possible Worlds Semantics' (Note 7 above), pp. 307–308. Relatively little of the total force of the Frege Principle is needed for this one purpose, however.

[14] See the different papers of mine collected in *Game-Theoretical Semantics*, ed. by Esa Saarinen, D. Reidel, Dordrecht and Boston, 1978.

[15] Cf. 'Theories of Meaning', p. 387: ". . . we must be able to specify, in a way that depends effectively and solely on formal considerations, what every sentence means".

[16] See 'Quantifiers vs Quantification Theory', *Linguistic Inquiry* **5** (1974), 153–177; reprinted in Saarinen, editor (Note 13 above).

[17] 'Quantifiers in Natural Languages: Some Logical Problems II', *Philosophy and Linguistics* **1** (1977), 153–172; reprinted in Saarinen (Note 14 above).

[18] See Esa Saarinen, 'Backwards-Looking Operators in Tense Logic and in Natural Language', *Reports from the Department of Philosophy, University of Helsinki*, No. 4, 1977; 'Intentional Identity Interpreted', *ibid.*, No. 5; 'Propositional Attitudes, Anaphora, and Backwards-Looking Operators', *ibid.*, No. 6. The first of these will also appear in *Essays in Mathematical and Philosophical Logic*, ed. by Jaakko Hintikka, Ilkka Niiniluoto, and Esa Saarinen, D. Reidel, Dordrecht, 1978, and the second in *Philosophy and Linguistics*.

[19] This idea was first mentioned in Lauri Carlson and Jaakko Hintikka, 'Conditionals, Generic Quantifiers, and Other Applications of Subgames', in *Meaning and Use*, ed. by Avishai Margalit, D. Reidel, Dordrecht, 1978; reprinted in Saarinen (ed.), Note 14 above.

[20] This phenomenon marks one of the most interesting and most neglected differences between formal and natural languages. I have mentioned it earlier in 'Quantifiers in Natural Language' (Note 17 above).

[21] See the paper mentioned in Note 19 above.

[22] See, for instance, Jon Barwise, *Admissible Sets and Structures*, Springer-Verlag, Berlin-Heidelberg-New York, 1975.

[23] See their paper, 'A New Approach to Infinitary Languages', *Annals of Mathematical Logic* **10** (1976), 95–115, and cf. Juha Oikkonen, 'Second Order Definability, Game Quantifiers, and Related Expressions', *Societas Scientiarum Fennica, Commentationes Physico-Mathematicae* **48** (1978), 39–101.

[24] See Leon Henkin, 'Some Remarks on Infinitely Long Formulas', in *Infinististic Methods*

(no editor given), (Pergamon Press, London, 1961); H. B. Enderton, 'Finite Partially-Ordered Quantifiers', *Zeitschrift für mathematische Logik und Grundlagen der Mathematik* **16** (1970), 393–397; W. Walkoe, Jr., 'Finite Partially Ordered Quantification', *Journal of Symbolic Logic* **35** (1970), 535–550; Jon Barwise, 'Some Applications of Henkin Quantifiers', *Israel Journal of Mathematics* **25** (1976), 47–63.

[25] See Jon Barwise, 'On Branching Quantifiers in English', *Journal of Philosophical Logic* **8** (1979), 47–80, esp. Appendix 5.

[26] See 'Quantifiers vs Quantification Theory' (Note 16 above) and 'Quantifiers in Natural Languages: Some Logical Problems I', in *Essays on Mathematical and Philosophical Logic*, ed. by Jaakko Hintikka, Ilkka Niiniluoto, and Esa Saarinen (D. Reidel, Dordrecht, 1978); both reprinted in Saarinen, editor (Note 14 above).

[27] Ray S. Jackendoff, *Semantic Interpretation in Generative Grammar* (MIT Press, Cambridge, Mass., 1972). (See pp. 305–308.)

[28] *The Semantics of Questions and the Questions of Semantics* (*Acta Philosophica Fennica* **28,** No. 4), North-Holland, Amsterdam, 1976, esp. Chapters 6, 8–9.

[29] Cf. Dummett, *Frege* (Note 6 above), pp. 186–192.

[30] Carnap's discussion in *Meaning and Necessity* (University of Chicago Press, Chicago, 1956), pp. 121–124 comes very close to this identification.

[31] Frege's own formulations sometimes encourage such a view; cf. 'Sinn und Bedeutung', pp. 37–38, 49–50 of the original. We read for instance on p. 37: "One can legitimately conclude only that the reference of a sentence is *not always* its truth-value'.

[32] Cf., e.g., the articles collected in my books *Models for Modalities* (D. Reidel, Dordrecht, 1969) and *The Intentions of Intentionality* (D. Reidel, Dordrecht, 1975), esp. the paper 'Carnap's Heritage in Logical Semantics'.

[33] See the papers listed in Note 2 above, esp. 'In Defense of Convention T'.

[34] I am employing Quinean quasi-quotes (corner quotes) in the T-schema and its derivatives.

[35] See Jaakko Hintikka, 'A Counterexample to Tarski-Type Truth Definitions as Applied to Natural Languages', *Philosophia* **5** (1975), 207–212; 'The Prospects for Convention T', *Dialectica* **30** (1976), 61–66.

[36] Cf. James C. Klagge, 'Convention T Regained', *Philosophical Studies* **32** (1977), 377–381.

[37] See Jaakko Hintikka, 'Quantifiers in Natural Languages: Some Logical Problems II' (Note 17 above).

[38] Alex Blum, 'Convention T and Natural Languages', *Dialectica* **32** (1978), 77–80.

[39] This paper began its life as my intended contribution to the Reidel *Profiles* volume on Donald Davidson, but it soon grew far too long to be acceptable for that purpose. I have not tried to eliminate the obvious signs of its early history, however. Much of the work that has gone into it was supported by a John Simon Guggenheim Memorial Foundation Fellowship for 1979–80.

BARBARA HALL PARTEE

MONTAGUE GRAMMAR, MENTAL REPRESENTATIONS, AND REALITY*

1. INTRODUCTION

Over the past ten years or so, there has been a notable convergence of interest between linguists and philosophers on issues in semantic theory and the semantic description of natural languages. Within the line of development in which Montague's work is an important milestone, a key feature has been the influence of the formal semantic theories of logicians on the semantic analysis of natural languages, and the equally important influence of natural language semantic description on the elaboration and enrichment of formal semantic theories. Although this development is in many ways similar to the development of syntax under Chomsky and other generative grammarians in the past two decades, a development marked at least at the outset by the mutual influence of progressively refined formal syntactic theories and progressively formalized syntactic descriptions of natural language phenomena, nevertheless there remains considerable skepticism among some linguists toward the applicability of formal logical models to natural language semantics. In my own previous work I have argued for the appropriateness of a suitably constrained Montague-type possible worlds semantics as a candidate for a linguistic theory of semantics; in this paper I wish to raise what I perceive to be certain fundamental problems in the application of Montague's theory to the goals of linguistics.

In particular, I will begin by setting out three claims; the first two claims, if jointly correct, indicate that there is an important problem, and the third, if correct, suggests that the solution will not be simple. A good bit of the paper is devoted to establishing that there is a problem and attempting to elucidate its nature and its sources; the final part of the paper does not, alas, contain the solution; but I will suggest certain lines of attack and attempt to assess their prospects.

The three claims, in their roughest and boldest form, are the following:

(i) If a natural language, e.g. English, is constituted in part by its syntax and semantics, then on Montague's theory of syntax and semantics English is such that no native speaker of

S. Kanger and S. Öhman (eds.), Philosophy and Grammar, 59–78.

English can know English.

(ii) On the Chomskyan view of language and grammar, a language is defined by its grammar and a grammar is a human mental construct, so a native speaker of a given language must by definition know his or her language.

(iii) The conflict between (i) and (ii) arises from a difference in conception of what semantics is, a difference which is crucial particularly at the lexical level.

It may be that the conflict arises *only* at the level of lexical semantics, although I suspect and will suggest below that it is also relevant to the problem of the semantics of propositional attitude constructions. But at the outset I will concentrate on the conflict at the lexical level, and I will begin by contrasting syntax and "structural" semantics with lexical semantics.

I should note before going further that my views on these matters have been strongly influenced by those of Hilary Putnam, and that the problem I have stated by means of assertions (i)–(iii) above is very similar to that expressed by Putnam as follows:

> So theory of meaning came to rest on two unchallenged assumptions:
> (I) That knowing the meaning of a term is just a matter of being in a certain psychological state.
> (II) That the meaning of a term (in the sense of 'intension') determines its extension (in the sense that sameness of intension determines sameness of extension.)
>
> I shall argue that these two assumptions are not jointly satisfied by *any* notion, let alone any notion of meaning.[1]

Now I do not believe that Montague ever held the first of Putnam's assumptions, nor that Chomsky would endorse the second, so one might respond to the conflict by suggesting that linguistic semantics and philosophical semantics of Montague's sort are simply two distinct enterprises,[2] and that it is misguided to try to apply a theory like Montague's to linguistic goals. Part of my aim is then to argue that at the structural level, Montague's approach *is* compatible with the goals of linguistic theory, so there is good reason to want to try to resolve the incompatibility at the lexical level.

2. SYNTACTIC AND SEMANTIC STRUCTURES

The central task of syntax is to give a finite description of the infinite set of sentences of a given natural language. The basic observation underlying the acceptance of this task as central is that the native speaker of a language can produce and understand sentences he or she has never produced or encountered before, that there is in principle no upper bound on the length of sentences, and that the brain is finite. The form of a solution to this task, agreed on by linguists and philosophers alike,[3] is to specify the finite set of lexical items of the language and a finite set of syntactic rules which, taken together, generate the infinite set of sentences. Although there are conflicting theories about the detailed nature of the lexicon, all of them involve a basis of a finite stock of elements which the native speaker must simply learn in effect as a list.

For what I would call the structural part of semantics, or alternatively the question of 'logical form', the central problem is perfectly analogous to the central task of syntax: to give a finite description of the *meanings* of the infinite set of sentences of the language. And again, in spite of differences about what meanings are and many differences of detail, there is general agreement that the same kind of solution is appropriate: one should explicitly give the meanings of the finite set of lexical items, and give a finite set of rules for assigning meanings to complex expressions on the basis of the meanings of their parts. For those working on the structural part, there is in general an explicit or implicit assumption that the lexical part is at bottom simply a list, as it is in syntax.[4] I will say more below about the consequences of differing views about the form and content of the specification of the meanings of the basic elements, but what I want to emphasize at this point is that when one takes as central the question of how meanings are associated with the infinite set of sentences of a language, one is naturally led to concentrate on the recursive devices that make for the infinitude of the language, and to attribute to the finite set of basic elements just whatever is needed for them to provide appropriate inputs to the recursive rules.

This strategy or working hypothesis can be seen very clearly, for example, in Montague's treatments of fragments of English. Montague took the basic aim of semantics to be the characterization of the notions of a true sentence (under a given interpretation) and of entailment,[5] and took as a starting point Frege's distinction between intension and extension. Then, given the basic Fregean thesis (which may be variously formulated[6]) that the intension of a complex expression is a function of the intensions of its parts, while the extension of an expression is not always a function of the extensions of the parts, but is always a function of the extensions and intensions of its parts, it is natural that Montague's semantic rules start with the intensions of basic lexical items as givens, since the intensions are needed as inputs to the semantic rules and the intensions cannot be determined from the extension at any one world.

If one takes the stipulation of the intensions of the basic lexical items as a starting point, a great deal of substantive work with empirically testable consequences can be and has been done to provide the rules for semantically interpreting complex expressions. Consider a typical higher-level construction such as the combination of a common noun phrase with a restrictive relative clause, or the construction of an attributive adjective with a common noun; a semantic interpretation rule for such a construction makes predictions about an infinite class of expressions, and these predictions can be tested for correctness with respect to truth conditions and entailment relations without the need to consider anything of the semantic content of particular lexical items besides their logical type. Work of this kind has been carried on by both linguists and philosophers, and with the exception perhaps of the problem of propositional attitudes, there is no evidence of conflict between Montague's methods and the linguists' goals in this area: the rules for combining interpretations of parts to make interpretations for wholes are finitely representable and correspond as far as one can tell with the intuitions of native speakers, and there seems to be no difficulty in principle in saying that the speakers of a language 'know' these rules as part of their competence.

Thomason (1974) underscores the separability of lexical and structural semantics and goes further in his introduction to Montague (1974):

> The problems of semantic theory should be distinguished from those of lexicography. . . . A central goal of [semantics] is to explain how different kinds of meanings attach to different syntactic categories; another is to explain how the meanings of phrases depend on those of their components. . . . *But we should not expect a semantic theory to furnish an account of how any two expressions belonging to the same syntactic category differ in meaning*. 'Walk' and 'run', for instance, and 'unicorn' and 'zebra' certainly do differ in meaning, and we require a dictionary of English to tell us how. But the making of a dictionary demands considerable knowledge of the world. . . . These are matters of application, not of theory. (pp. 48–49, emphasis Thomason's).

I disagree with Thomason's choice of the 'application vs theory' terminology here; but I agree with the idea that lexical semantics is a fundamentally different kind of enterprise from structural semantics (which Thomason calls simply 'semantics'). I also sympathize with the spirit of Thomason's remark in the same passage that it would be unfair to require a theoretician studying structural semantics to simultaneously solve all the problems of lexical semantics. But I believe it *is* fair to raise questions concerning the assumptions about lexical semantics presupposed by Montague's structural theory if these assumptions bear directly on the question of whether a speaker of a language can know his language.

3. THE PROBLEM OF THE PRIMITIVES AT THE LEXICAL LEVEL

A. *Linguists' Views*

I think it is fair to say that most generative linguists have held that semantic primitives, like syntactic primitives, are basically mental constructs. Jackendoff (1972) writes,

> To suppose a universal semantic representation is to make an important claim about the innateness of semantic structure. The semantic representation, it is reasonable to hope, is very tightly integrated into the cognitive system of the human mind (p. 1).

Katz (1972) takes a more Fregean view of his own semantic markers, saying that

> a semantic marker is a theoretical construct which is intended to represent a concept. . . . [Concepts] are not . . . elements in the subjective process of thinking, but rather the objective content of thought processes. (p. 38).

Nevertheless, Katz does hold that these semantic representations, if not themselves mental entities, are knowable: "A speaker's ability to understand any sentence depends in part on his knowing the meanings of its component morphemes" (p. 35). Linguists are recently coming to acknowledge the importance of the interplay of the 'language faculty' with other parts of the human cognitive and perceptual apparatus, as is evidenced, for example, by recent attention to the fact that the universality of what are taken to be the clearest cases of basic color terms such as 'red' can be linked to properties of the visual color receptors themselves.[7] One might say, perhaps too simplistically, that on the linguists' view, if there are semantic relations between linguistic expressions and non-linguistic, non-mental entities, these relations are mediated by human cognitive and perceptual constructs, and the 'semantic representations' that the linguist hypothesizes are to be ultimately grounded in psychological states and processes. The centrality of psychological notions is in turn, I believe, a natural result of Chomsky's stress on linguistic competence as the central object of linguistic study:

> Why study language? . . . by studying language we may discover abstract principles that govern its structure and use, principles that are universal by biological necessity and not mere historical accident, that derive from mental characteristics of the species . . . . [Language] is a product of human intelligence, created anew in each individual by operations that lie far beyond the reach of will or consciousness (Chomsky 1975, p. 4).

B. Possible Worlds Semantics

On the possible worlds semantics approach as exemplified by Montague, lexical semantics is a matter of specifying a particular intensional model which includes an assignment of a particular intension to each basic lexical item. The intension is a function from possible worlds to objects of the appropriate type, a function which picks out the extension of the lexical item in each possible world. Several points bear emphasis:

(i) Montague's treatments of English do not specify a unique intensional model for the fragment of English; rather, he provides a family of models which can differ with respect to any or all of the parameters which make up an intensional model: a set A of individuals, a set I of possible worlds, a set J of moments of time, and the interpretation function F which assigns intensions to basic lexical items. Meaning postulates may be added to restrict the class of admissible models, but even that addition simply pares the set of models down to what Montague calls the 'logically possible interpretations', a determination sufficient for the logical notions of logical truth, logical implication, and logical equivalence.

(ii) The alternative specifications of the interpretation function F in the model amount to alternative 'possible dictionaries'. As Montague remarks in 'English as a Formal Language',

> The use of a language would ideally involve not only the determination of the collection of *all* models of the language . . ., but also the specification of a particular, actual model; this would be involved in characterizing *absolute* truth (as opposed to truth with respect to a model) (p. 209 in Montague, 1974).

Note that this lexical indeterminacy does not infect the structural part of the semantics; the principles for determining the interpretations of complex expressions from their parts are stated in a uniform way, so that their application does not require knowing any of the particular meanings of the parts.

(iii) The variations in thc sets A and I across models represent alternative metaphysics; I believe that Montague, like David Lewis, takes a realist position with respect to the existence of a 'correct' choice for A and I. If knowing a language required knowing what all the possible worlds and possible individuals really are, then certainly no human knows any language. But it is usual to separate out that aspect of the models by requiring only that for a speaker to know the meaning of a sentence, he must know, *given* any possible world, whether the sentence is true or false in that world.[8] Then the fact that a person may never be able to apprehend or 'be given' a complete specification of a possible world need not count against his *linguistic* competence.

Let us consider, then, what it would take to specify a particular actual model for English or a fragment of it, in particular what it would take to fix the lexicon by a particular interpretation function F. It is at this point that Putnam's arguments are central and the conflict between the psychologistic and non-psychologistic views of semantics becomes apparent.

4. FIXING THE ACTUAL INTERPRETATION FUNCTION

Kripke[9] has argued persuasively that proper names are 'rigid designators', which pick out the same individual in every possible world; which individual a certain name refers to depends on the causal history of the use of the name, tracing back to something like an original 'dubbing', an act typically involving a demonstrative or ostensive reference to a particular real-world object. If we accept this view, then clearly the intension of a proper name is not fixed by any common representation in the heads of the speakers who use the name as part of their language. But this example alone is not taken as very central to issues of semantic representation by most linguists; Katz, for instance, simply argues that proper names do not have any meaning.[10] (It would seem to follow from Katz's compositional principles that sentences containing proper nouns should not have any meaning either; I do not know whether Katz has any solution to that apparent inadequacy of his proposal.)

Putnam has argued in a number of articles that a similar process is involved in a great many cases; he focusses particularly on 'natural kind' terms such as names of biological species[11], diseases, and physical phenomena such as electricity and magnetism. The successful introduction of a term like 'tiger' typically includes two primary factors: (i) an ostensive reference to one or more tigers,[12] and (ii) a correct supposition by the original user of the term that those individuals are instances of a natural kind, say a biological species. Typical users of the term will have at their psychological disposal at most certain criteria or a 'stereotype' for identifying tigers, not in general sufficient to distinguish tigers from other possible species with similar outward appearances, yet because of the causal history of the term in the language, it will continue to refer to the actual species involved in the original introduction of the term.

In general we may say that for every term whose introduction into English depended in part on a demonstrative or ostensive 'reference-fixing' act, the intension of the term is determined in part by properties of the real-world object(s) involved in the original introduction of the term. In such cases, human ignorance about the extension of the term and/or about the causal history of its use leads to ignorance about the intension, without preventing the term from *having* the appropriate intension in the language used by the speaker. In this respect it makes perfect sense, and is probably true, to say that a speaker of a language does not in general fully *know* his language. (We will discuss below the question of how communication is ordinarily not impaired by this deficit.)

But there is nevertheless a psychological factor whose importance Putnam may have underestimated. He hints at it in one passage:[13]

> Of course, even in the light of later theory, the 'boundaries' of the kind in question may require more or less arbitrary legislation: in *this* sense *some* stipulation may have entered into the present technical definition.

I think the issue of the 'boundaries' of most terms is more central than this. In the case of ordinary proper names, we are dealing with the sorts of real-world referents for which we have the best grip on boundaries; problems with individuation and reidentification of persons are rare in actual practice and arise for the most part only in philosophical discussion. For biological species, the situation is almost as good, but it is clear that one cannot name a whole species simply by dubbing an individual member of the species with a name; there must also be the supposition that the individual is an example of the species and the intention to apply the name to the whole species, with the attendant problems of distinguishing species from subspecies, etc. A theory of species provides in effect a kind of similarity basis for extending the application of the term to other actual and possible exemplars.

For many terms of a natural language, there is much less of a theory available or imaginable for setting the boundaries involved in extending the application of the term from an original set of examples to a determinate extension and intension. Consider, for example, words describing kinds of houses: *cottage, mansion, bungalow, ranch, Cape Cod, Victorian*, etc.; the distinctions marked by such words depend on largely accidental facts about co-occurrences of properties across actual houses, and to the extent that their intensions are at all sharp, it is undoubtedly in large part the result of the disposition of language users to make similar inductive generalizations from similar experience. In this case there may be relevant 'experts', the realtors and architects, who play a role akin to that described by Putnam for the biologists with species names, the chemists with names of elements, etc.[14] But then what about words with evaluational content like *gentle, kind, mean, friendly, boring, spiteful*, etc.? For such words there are no experts, and there is no prospect of a theory of their 'real' natures; there is probably *only* a shared disposition to certain inductive generalizations.

I would sum up the importance of the psychological contribution to meaning as follows: for every term whose introduction and transmission in the language depends in part on induction from instances, the extension and intension are both indeterminate to the extent that there is no unique best similarity basis for the induction, and the disposition of speakers to make similar inductions from similar experience is crucial to the term's being determinate enough to be communicatively useful.

Kathleen Dahlgren, in an interesting recent paper,[15] supports Putnam's insistence on the role of the actual extension in the determination of meaning with a discussion of the influence of historical social change on the change in extension and meaning of a family of terms denoting social rank. She examines the history of social structure and of words denoting social rank in the Anglo-Saxon period and around the time of the Norman Conquest, and attests many instances where "shift in the properties of the extension of [an individual lexical item] lead to semantic shift" (p. 23). For example, the word which is the ancestor of modern English *churl* underwent a shift from something like 'the lowest rank of freeman' (690 AD) to 'semiserf' (1050 AD) to 'serf' (1100 AD), including in the last shift something which in terms of Katzian semantic markers would have to be represented as a shift from a semantic marker (Free) to its negation ($\overline{\text{Free}}$), and many other changes in the sort of associated 'conceptual content' which both decomposition analyses and meaning postulate approaches tend to try to capture. The sense in which one can say in such a case that the extension has stayed fixed and its *properties* have shifted, rather than saying that extension and meaning are shifting together, is not discussed by Dahlgren. I think a satisfactory answer in the spirit of Putnam can be given: that the extension is in this case determined by membership in a social class which persists as an entity despite continual replacements in its membership, much as our bodies persist through changes of individual atoms and molecules. (Such a description would probably not apply to a social structure where social class membership was more mobile, but social rank terms would probably be less nearly rigid in such cases.)

But in spite of the importance of recognizing the role of the actual extension in fixing the meaning of the term, I believe that Dahlgren's examples equally clearly point up the importance of the contribution of the cognitive propensities of native speakers: a still earlier meaning of the word *ceorl* was simply 'man', and a meaning which followed all of the social class meanings is essentially the present one, 'rude, low-bred fellow'.[16] The shift between the use of the term to designate a social rank and its use to designate something else, such as a personality trait or manner of social behavior, involves a shift in the perceived similarity basis for carrying out the induction from a given set of examples to a wider range of application. One can never (or only in marginal cases) ostensively display the entire extension of a predicate; and the similarity relation involved in generalizing from an example to a whole extension is not always subject to scientific investigation, as it is in Putnam's natural kind example. In the case of words like *aggressive, gentle, kind*, etc., there is no appropriate generic term to put into an ostensive definition in the way Putnam puts 'liquid' into the ostensive definition of 'water', i.e. 'this liquid is called water'. The best one might do is something vague like 'this manner of behaving is called aggressive', but the relation 'same manner of behaving as' is wildly indeterminate; there is nothing 'out there' in the real world to give a basis for a correct theory of manners of behaving, so our shared dispositions to perceive similarity in the same way are crucial.

The conclusion I draw from these observations is that the fixing of the interpretation of lexical items almost always involves *both* "the actual nature of the particular things that serve as paradigms" (Putnam 1975b, p. 245), which is independent of and not fully knowable by the users of the language, *and* the shared perceptual and cognitive properties of the human mind which contribute to determining the nature of the generalization of which the paradigms are taken to serve as instances.

I spoke of fixing the interpretation; Putnam speaks of fixing the extension and argues against intensions, and Dahlgren takes her extension of Putnam's arguments as arguments for a 'referential' as opposed to 'intensional' semantics. But both of them base their arguments on a use of the term 'intension' which views intensions as things in people's heads. (Dahlgren's arguments are really directed against Katz, who views his semantic representations as intensions and as known by speakers; in that respect I agree with Dahlgren completely.) But on Kripke's or Montague's use of the term 'intension', which does *not* treat intensions as mental entities, I see no conflict between the account just given of how interpretations are fixed and the view that interpretations are intensions. What fixes the extension also fixes the intension.

When a term like 'horse' was introduced, at most a small subset of the then existing horses were historically connected to the linguistic act. The same factors which account for the correctness of the term's application to the rest of the then existing horses account for its application to subsequently born horses and equally to the many possible horses that would have been born had things gone differently. The effect of the actual nature of the objects involved in the introduction of a term is to make its intension partly rigid, in the sense in which Kripke's treatment of proper names makes their intensions entirely rigid. Note in this regard the sharp contrast between the possible-worlds semantic approach and Katz's approach with respect to proper names: Katz says they have no meaning, where Kripke says they have an intension which simply picks out the same object in every possible world. Both are agreed that what's in the speaker's head does not determine the reference; only if intensions are required to be mental entities does that prevent the intension from determining the extension.

5. SEMANTIC COMPETENCE

We have come around to the view that the intensions of lexical items are not mental entities and are not fixed by psychological properties of language users. For a philosopher in the logical tradition like Montague or Thomason, such a conclusion is in no way problematical, since semantics in that tradition has always been the study of the relation between expressions in a language and the non-linguistic subject matter that the expressions are about, and not a study of the relation between linguistic expressions and the internalized rules and representations which make up the competence of language users. But for the linguist, it may seem intitially to be a paradoxical conclusion: the intensions of the lexical items, like the rest of the semantics and syntax, must be fixed for a particular language by the users of the language,since natural languages are a human creation, differ from one another, and change over time. Intensions themselves, the functions from possible worlds to objects of various sorts, are abstract objects which can exist independently of humans, like numbers; but what determines that a particular intension is the intension of a particular lexical item in a particular natural language must depend on facts about that natural language, and hence must depend on properties of the speakers of the language.

There is, I believe, a clear way out of this apparent paradox, based on the 'causal history' ideas that have been stressed by Kripke and Donnellan[17] and on the 'socio-linguistic hypothesis' about the 'division of linguistic labor' advanced by Putnam. It *is* properties of the users of a language that determine what the actual interpretations of the lexical items in the language are, but it is not just their narrowly psychological properties that matter. Equally important are the interactions of the speakers with the external world that accompany the introduction of words into the language, and the socially indispensable intentions of the speakers to use their words in the same way. The fact that it was H_2O and not XYZ in the samples that were in a certain relation to the speaker when the word 'water' was introduced is one factor in fixing the intension of 'water'; and this factor crucially involves the speaker, not just the water and the word, since without the original speaker's intention to *use* the word to refer to the stuff in those samples, the word 'water' in English would not refer to that stuff. So the properties of the speakers who introduce words into the language are crucial, but not just their psychological properties. Now what about the other speakers and the later transmission of the language? Chomsky likens language acquisition to language creation; in syntax, for example, the child must construct a grammar on the basis of the language use of the surrounding community and his own innate 'acquisition device', and if the members of a new generation for whatever reason construct a grammar that differs from that of their predecessors, the syntax of the language simply changes: the first 'creators' of the syntax have no privileged status. I believe this is one of the most crucial differences between syntax and structural semantics on the one hand and lexical semantics on the other: in the latter case, the circumstances surrounding the introduction of a term into the language usually *do* make a distinctive contribution to the extension and intension of the term.

The transmission of a lexical item through a language, across speakers and across time, crucially involves a social cooperative intention to speak the same language. In principle, a speaker could introduce a word to refer rigidly to a particular object, that object could then go out of existence and leave no traces of any sort, and the word could stay in the language and continue to refer rigidly to that object, even though no other speakers were in anything like the situation of the speaker who introduced the term, simply by virtue of the fact that the other speakers are in implicit agreement to use the word to refer to whatever it was used to refer to by whoever they learned it from. In practice, a word whose intension was that ephemeral would not be likely to survive because it would not be very useful for communicative purposes. And the fact that the intensions of words do change across time indicates that the transmission process is not as entirely passive as my extreme example suggests.[18]

If we consider what goes on in the process of the acquisition of lexical items, I think we can begin to account both for the way in which a speaker can come to be a competent user of words whose intensions he does not really know and for the fact that during the transmission process words do sometimes come to acquire different intensions. There are two main ways in which the language learner finds out something about the intensions of words: through language-to-language grounding and language-to-world grounding. The language-to-language grounding comes basically by accepting certain sentences as true, particularly such sentences as are perceived to be regarded by the community of language users as most impervious to challenge by empirical evidence, e.g. 'Bachelors are unmarried males'. Both meaning postulates of the Carnapian sort and the lexical decomposition analyses of Katz, Jackendoff, and many other linguists can be taken as encoding generally shared beliefs about relations among the intensions of various words. (Some of these beliefs may be false but useful – e.g. 'Whales are fish' could help a learner with the acquisition of 'whale', just as a false identifying description can often help a hearer determine which individual a speaker is referring to.) But as Richard Grandy[19] and others have pointed out, no amount of such intralinguistic connections can serve to tie down the intensions with respect to their extralinguistic content.[20] For that there must be some language-to-world grounding; this is the part of lexical semantics that has no analog in syntax or structural semantics and where the interconnections among language, thought, and reality are perhaps most complex.

One could imagine a youngster in a community of omniscient gods learning the intensions of words directly by ostension: an adult god could perhaps 'point to' a particular function from all possible worlds to objects or sets of the appropriate sort, and say '*that* is the intension of "glark"'. But humans are limited in many crucial ways that put strong limitations on the possibility of 'grasping' intensions. Suppose speaker A has introduced a new word, say 'horse', into the language and wants to transmit it to speaker B. For a word with such a high degree of 'real-world' content, speaker A might well try to get speaker B into a situation similar to that in which the introduction of the term occurred, and say something like '*That* kind of animal is called a *horse*'. Speaker A himself, as we have argued, does not *know* the intension of 'horse', and the intension is furthermore indeterminate with respect to the many different generalizations that could be made from the original example under the rubric of 'same kind of animal'. In the transmission process as exemplified in this case, there are at least the following limiting factors: (i) the sample appealed to in transmission will in general be different from the sample involved in the original naming; (ii) only certain properties of the sample are accessible to the speakers, generally the perceptually salient properties; the non-linguistic objects that enter into fixing the intensions of terms enter into the determination of the speaker's understanding of those intensions only via the speaker's perceptual system and associated belief structure, i.e. the speaker is never directly 'given' even a sample of the extension; (iii) even in an imaginary case where speaker A and speaker B could somehow be 'given' the same sample and given direct knowledge of it, the basically inductive problem would remain: the determination of the way the intension of the term is meant to generalize from the sample. If there is a correct theory of biological species, and the intension of 'species' is already fixed in accordance with such a theory, the direction of generalization from sample can be tied down for the intension of 'horse' by saying 'animals of this *species* are called horses'. But in the normal case of language transmission neither speaker A nor speaker B has access to enough of such a theory for the intension to be *psychologically* fixed by such a process.

Quine (1974) has discussed many of the reasons why language transmission succeeds as well as it does in the face of such potential obstacles; as he puts it, "our innate standards of perceptual similarity show a gratifying tendency to run with the grain of nature. This concurrence is accountable, surely, to natural selection" (p. 19). And later,

We may expect our innate similarity standards to be much alike, since they are hereditary in the race; and even as these standards gradually change with experience we may expect them to stay significantly alike, what with our shared environment, shared culture, shared language, and mutual influence.

(In adopting this kind of explanation from Quine, who does not accept the notion of intensions as a useful one, I am depending on my earlier argument that the fixing of intensions is really the same as the process of fixing extensions.) So it is basically the congruence of both our perceptual similarity standards and our inductive propensities with both nature and each other's that enables us, if not to 'grasp' intensions, to attain enough knowledge about them to communicate with each other and to be able to use sentences whose truth-conditions are not determinable on the basis of our internal psychological states.

Let me return to another point which I introduced above, concerning language change. In the process of language transmission described above, one of the limitations mentioned was in the process of induction from a sample application of a term to its wider application. It is primarily because of the indeterminacy of this process that I believe the intensions of most words in natural language are not really sharply fixed, and I believe this has a great deal to do with the historical changes that occur in lexical semantics. Putnam has focussed on natural kind terms to emphasize the role that non-psychological, real-world factors play in fixing the interpretation of lexical items, and one may note that such terms are among the most stable historically. If one focusses on non-natural kind terms such as the social rank terms discussed by Dahlgren, or terms for describing personality characteristics or political views, the kinds of inductive generalization that can be made from a given sample of application are much less sharply determined either by facts about how the world is or by our innate similarity standards; both the original introducers of the term and those to whom it is transmitted are likely not to go beyond something as vague as 'like such-and-such a sample' with respect to personality, political views, etc. When the terms are not about things for which there could be a scientific theory, then there is no basis for saying that their intensions *are* completely fixed, either by the intentions of the speakers or by 'the correct theory' of the objects in the original sample of the extension. It still does not follow that the intensions in such cases are to be *equated* with psychological properties of the language users in such cases, but the psychological factors are then much greater, and the combination of changes in the properties of the sample and consequent changes in the inductions the language users make from the sample can readily lead to changes in the intension itself.

Contrast, for example, the natural kind word 'electricity', which Putnam argues convincingly has not changed its reference (nor, we may add, its intension), in spite of many shifts in scientific theory, with Dahlgren's example 'churl' when it went from applying to members of a particular social class to a predicate expressing a certain manner of social behavior. Electricity itself hasn't changed over the centuries, while social class structure has; and social class structure itself is in part determined by psychological facts in a way that electricity is not. Earlier and later users of the term 'electricity' can be said to be referring to the same thing; the same does not hold for the earlier and later users of 'churl', and it seems best to say that the intension in that case did change.

On the basis of these considerations about the difference between intensions and what's in people's heads, one could argue for the appropriateness of the linguistic term 'semantic representation' by putting it in a slightly different framework than linguists usually do. The competent speaker of a language does not know the intensions of his words, we have argued, but this is very much like, and closely related to, the fact that he does not know everything about the world he lives in. To operate competently within the world certainly does not require 'knowing' the world; but humans do presumably internalize a great many beliefs and perceptions about the world, which we could call 'world representations', and the structure of our conceptions of the world is a rich area of investigtion for cognitive psychology. If 'semantic representations' were similarly viewed as psychological constructs which reflect our beliefs and perceptions about the semantics of our language, and not as *being* the semantics, the conflict between the psychologistic and non-psychologistic views of semantics would be greatly reduced. This requires, however, that one accept the ideas that the lexical items of a language have intensions, that this association of lexical items and intensions is part of the semantics of a language, and that what the intensions of the lexical items are is not determinable from purely psychological properties of the competent users of the language. This, as I have said before, makes lexical semantics very different from syntax, since what the syntax of a natural language is *is* determinable, I believe, from the psychological states of its users.

6. LANGUAGE AS A 'WINDOW ON THE MIND'

I have stressed the claim, originally argued for by Putnam, that meanings of lexical items are not in speakers' heads. I have also stressed that in this respect, lexical semantics is fundamentally different from syntax and structural semantics. Let me conclude with a few suggestions and possible morals for linguistic and philosophical semantics.

First, and perhaps of narrowest interest, is the conclusion that Montague was not wrong to make semantic interpretations be a kind of thing that could not be in a speaker's head. In his framework, the syntactic and structural semantic rules are finitely representable and intuitively plausible, and it is only the intensional models that are not directly cognitively accessible. This opens up a domain of psychological inquiry to investigate the internalized representations by means of which we can operate with the intensions of lexical items without directly 'knowing' them, a domain of inquiry potentially similar to the psychology of logic or mathematics. Insofar as linguists are inclined to view linguistics as a branch of psychology, such inquiries may hold more interest for many linguists than the study of the intensional models themselves, but there is no reason why the two sorts of studies should not be compatible.

Secondly, and most speculatively, there is a possible implication from the separation of intensions from speakers' 'representations' of intensions to the problem of propositional attitude sentences. Many of the problems of propositional attitude sentences stem, I believe, from the fact that beliefs about the intensions of words cannot be sharply separated from other beliefs. When we consider an assertion such as 'Many children believe that clouds are alive', there is no way to draw a sharp line between differences in the child's beliefs and ours about the nature of clouds and the causes of their motion on the one hand and differences between the child's beliefs and ours about the intensions of the terms 'cloud' and 'alive'. This is certainly not the only source of problems with propositional attitude contexts, but I believe it is a fundamental one. I do not so far see any way to proceed from this conviction to an adequate analysis of those constructions, but I think it is for this kind of reason that treating the objects of belief as built up from the 'actual' intensions cannot be correct.

Finally, I want to suggest that the study of lexical semantics, when sharply differentiated from structural semantics, offers an extremely rich avenue into the study of the mind of a sort very different from that most often emphasized by Chomsky. Chomsky and Putnam have argued at length about the postulation of an innate, highly specific system of mechanisms and principles employed by the human child in the acquisition of language, as proposed by Chomsky, as opposed to the employment by the child of more generally applicable learning principles. The best arguments for Chomsky's side are the sort that have come from syntax, where there seem to be highly specific universals like the transformational cycle, which are learned effortlessly by the child at a period when other learning tasks that are prime facie much simpler seem to present him with much greater difficulty. I think it may well be true that we have hereditarily acquired highly syntax-specific mental structure, and that the study of syntax can thus lead to insight into the structure of the mind in intricate and important ways. Human language is 'our code', and we may well be in part 'wired' for it much as bees are wired for their less complex honey dance. But the study of syntax (and the structural part of semantics) may for that very reason not lead so directly to hypotheses or insights about other equally important properties of the human mind, such as the ability to make inductive inferences and solve open-ended problems, or the development of notions of causation, action, time, will, freedom, etc. The study of the acquisition of lexical items and the psychological parts of the processes that go into the determination of what the intensions of the lexical items are and how we manage to come as close as we do to sharing a common language whose basic terms have relatively fixed intensions seems to me, though in many respects a harder and less sharply defined problem than the study of syntax, a problem whose importance for the understanding of mind is enormous.

University of Massachusetts, Amherst

NOTES

* I am grateful to Emmon Bach for much helpful discussion and support, and to the Center for Advanced Study in the Behavioral Sciences for the fellowship and supportive services which made the preparation of this paper possible; part of the funds for the Center fellowship came from the National Science Foundation and the Andrew W. Mellon Foundation. In addition, I wish to express my gratitude to the University of Uppsala, to Sten Carlsson, Dean of the Faculty of Arts, and to Professors Stig Kanger and Sven Öhman, for inviting me to participate in the symposium for which this paper was prepared and for the graciousness and excellent planning which made the occasion a stimulating and memorable one.

[1] Page 219 in Putnam (1975a); all page references to Putnam articles below are to that collection.
[2] Chomsky (1975).
[3] Not universally; cf. Hintikka (1975).
[4] See, for instance, Katz (1972), p. 36; Montague (1970a), pp. 189–191; Chomsky (1975), pp. 80–81.
[5] Montague (1970b), footnote 2.
[6] Montague took apparently different positions on this issue in Montague (1970a) and (1970b); David Lewis argues in Lewis (1974) that these and some other apparent alternatives are not substantively different from one another.
[7] For an interesting discussion of and contribution to the recent history of this topic, see Brown (1976).
[8] As emphasized, for instance, in Cresswell (forthcoming).
[9] See Kripke (1972).
[10] Katz (1972), pp. 381–382.
[11] For prime examples see Putnam (1975b, 1975c).
[12] The ostension involved may be indirect, e.g. 'the animal that left *these* pawprints', 'the germ that causes the disease that has *these* symptoms'.
[13] Putnam (1962), p. 312.
[14] But whereas the expert in biology may be engaged in trying to determine the essential properties of the various species as well as having sharper criteria for applying the species names to particular objects, the experts in housing styles are probably not in any better position than the average person to say which properties, if any, of bungalows are essential, rather they simply have sharper criteria of application.
[15] Dahlgren (1976).
[16] The glosses here are not intended as synonyms, but as contingently correct descriptions of the extensions of the terms.
[17] See for example Kripke (1972) and Donnellan (1974).
[18] Gareth Evans (1973) argues persuasively that even proper names can change their intensions over time (from a rigid destination of one individual to that of another), since what begins as a mistaken belief about the intension may, if it accumulates enough adherents, override the original act of dubbing.
[19] Grandy (1971).
[20] Meaning postulates may suffice for logical words like *and* which in a sense have no extralinguistic content.

BIBLIOGRAPHY

Brown, Roger: 1976, 'Reference: In Memorial Tribute to Eric Lenneberg', *Cognition* **4**, 125–153.

Chomsky, Noam: 1975, *Reflections on Language*, Pantheon Books, New York.

Cresswell, M. J.: (forthcoming), 'Semantic Competence', in M. Guenthner-Reuter and F. Guenthner (eds.), *Meaning and Translation: Philosophical and Linguistic Approaches*, Duckworth, London.

Dahlgren, Kathleen: 1976, 'Referential Semantics', in Joseph Emonds (ed.), *Proposals for*

Semantic and Syntactic Theory, UCLA Papers in Syntax, Vol. 7, Dept. of Linguistics, UCLA, Los Angeles.

Donnellan, Keith: 1974, 'Speaking of Nothing', *Philosophical Review* **83,** 3–32; reprinted in Schwartz (1977).

Evans, Gareth: 1973, 'The Causal Theory of Names', *Aristotelian Society Supplementary Volume* **47,** 187–208; reprinted in Schwartz (1977).

Grandy, Richard: 1971, 'Some Remarks on Logical Form', talk given at Eastern Division annual meeting of the Am. Phil. Assn.

Hintikka, Jaakko: 1975, 'On the Limitations of Generative Grammar', *Proceedings of the Scandinavian Seminar on Philosophy of Language*, Vol. I (1–92), Filosofiska Förening Filosofiska Institutionen vid Uppsala Universitet, Uppsala, Sweden.

Jackendoff, Ray: 1972, *Semantic Interpretation in Generative Grammar*, The MIT Press, Cambridge.

Katz, Jerrold J: 1972, *Semantic Theory*, Harper & Row, New York.

Kripke, Saul: 1972, 'Naming and Necessity', in D. Davidson and G. Harman (eds.), *Semantics of Natural Language*, D. Reidel, Dordrecht.

Lewis, David: 1974, ''Tensions', in M. Munitz and P. Unger (eds.), *Semantics and Philosophy*, NYU Press, New York, 49–61.

Montague, Richard: 1970a, 'English as a Formal Language', in B. Visentini *et al.*, *Linguaggi Nella Società e Nella Tecnica*, Edizioni di Comunità, Milan. Reprinted in Montague (1974).

Montague, Richard: 1970b, 'Universal Grammar', *Theoria* **36,** 373–98. Reprinted in Montague (1974).

Montague, Richard: 1973, 'The Proper Treatment of Quantification in Ordinary English', in K. J. J. Hintikka, J. M. E. Moravcsik, and P. Suppes (eds.), *Approaches to Natural Language: Proceedings of the 1970 Stanford Workshop on Grammar and Semantics*, D. Reidel, Dordrecht. Reprinted in Montague (1974).

Montague, Richard: 1974, *Formal Philosophy: Selected Papers of Richard Montague*, ed. and with an introduction by Richmond Thomason, Yale Univ. Press, New Haven.

Putnam, Hilary: 1962, 'Dreaming and "Depth Grammar" ', in R. Butler (eds.), *Analytical Philosophy First Series*, Oxford; reprinted in Putnam (1975a).

Putnam, Hilary: 1975a, *Mind, Language and Reality: Philosophical Papers*, Vol. 2, Cambridge University Press, Cambridge.

Putnam, Hilary: 1975b, 'The Meaning of "Meaning" ', in K. Gunderson (ed.), *Language Mind and Knowledge*, Minnesota Studies in the Philosophy of Science VII, University of Minnesota Press, Minneapolis. Reprinted in Putnam (1975a).

Putnam, Hilary: 1975c, 'Language and Reality', in Putnam (1975a).

Quine, W. V. O.: 1974, *The Roots of Reference*, Open Court, La Salle, Illinois.

Schwartz, Stephen P. (ed.): 1977, *Naming, Necessity, and Natural Kinds*, Cornell University Press, Ithaca.

Thomason, Richmond: 1974, 'Introduction', in Montague (1974).

DAVID LEWIS

INDEX, CONTEXT, AND CONTENT

1. SYNOPSIS

If a grammar is to do its jobs as part of a systematic restatement of our common knowledge about our practices of linguistic communication, it must assign semantic values that determine which sentences are true in which contexts. If the semantic values of sentences also serve to help determine the semantic values of larger sentences having the given sentence as a constituent, then also the semantic values must determine how the truth of a sentence varies when certain features of context are shifted, one feature at a time.

Two sorts of dependence of truth on features of context are involved: *context-dependence* and *index-dependence*. A *context* is a location – time, place, and possible world – where a sentence is said. It has countless features, determined by the character of the location. An *index* is an *n*-tuple of features of context, but not necessarily features that go together in any possible context. Thus an index might consist of a speaker, a time before his birth, a world where he never lived at all, and so on. Since we are unlikely to think of all the features of context on which truth sometimes depends, and hence unlikely to construct adequately rich indices, we cannot get by without context-dependence as well as index-dependence. Since indices but not contexts can be shifted one feature at a time, we cannot get by without index-dependence as well as context-dependence. An assignment of semantic values must give us the relation: sentence s is true at context c at index i, where i need not be the index that gives the features of context c. Fortunately, an index used together with a context in this way need not give all relevant features of context; only the shiftable features, which are much fewer.

Two alternative strategies are available. (1) Variable but simple semantic values: a sentence has different semantic values at different contexts, and these semantic values are functions from indices to truth values. (2) Complex but constant semantic values: a sentence has the same semantic value at all contexts, and this value is a function from context-index pairs to truth values. But the strategies are not genuine

S. Kanger and S. Öhman (eds.), Philosophy and Grammar, 79–100.

alternatives. They differ only superficially. Hence attempts to argue for the superiority of one over the other are misguided. Whatever one can do, the other can do, and with almost equal convenience.

2 PHILOSOPHY AND GRAMMAR

We have made it part of the business of philosophy to set down, in an explicit and systematic fashion, the broad outlines of our common knowledge about the practice of language. Part of this restatement of what we all know should run as follows. The foremost thing we do with words is to impart information, and this is how we do it. Suppose (1) that you do not know whether *A* or *B* or. . .; and (2) that I do know; and (3) that I want you to know; and (4) that no extraneous reasons much constrain my choice of words; and (5) that we both know that the conditions (1)–(5) obtain. Then I will be truthful and you will be trusting and thereby you will come to share my knowledge. I will find something to say that depends for its truth on whether *A* or *B* or . . . and that I take to be true. I will say it and you will hear it. You, trusting me to be willing and able to tell the truth, will then be in a position to infer whether *A* or *B* or. . . .

That was not quite right. Consider the tribe of Liars – the ones in the riddles, the folk we fear to meet at forks in the road. Unlike common liars, the Liars have no wish to mislead. They convey information smoothly to each other; and once we know them for what they are, we too can learn from them which road leads to the city. They are as truthful in their own way as we are in ours. But they are truthful in Liarese and we are truthful in English, and Liarese is a language like English but with all the truth values reversed. The missing part of my story concerns our knowledge that we are not of the tribe of Liars. I should not have spoken simply of my truthfulness and your trust. I should have said: I will be truthful-in-English and you will be trusting-in-English, and that is how you will come to share my knowledge. I will find something to say that depends for its truth-in-English on whether *A* or *B* or . . . and that I take to be true-in-English; you will trust me to be willing and able to tell the truth-in-English. Truthfulness-in-Liarese would have done as well (and truthfulness-in-English would not have done) had you been trusting-in-Liarese.

Truth-in-English – what is that? A complete restatement of our common knowledge about the practice of language may not use this phrase without explaining it. We need a chapter which culminates in a specification of the conditions under which someone tells the truth-in-English. I call that chapter a *grammar* for English.

I use the word 'grammar' in a broad sense. Else I could have found little to say about our assigned topic. If it is to end by characterizing truth-in-English, a grammar must cover most of what has been called syntax, much of what has been called semantics, and even part of the miscellany that has been called pragmatics. It must cover the part of pragmatics that might better have been called indexical semantics – pragmatics in the sense of Bar-Hillel [1] and Montague [10]. It need not cover some other parts of pragmatics: conversational appropriateness and implicature, disambiguation, taxonomy of speech acts, or what it is about us that makes some grammars right and others wrong.

I am proposing both a delineation of the subject of grammar and a modest condition of adequacy for grammars. A good grammar is one suited to play a certain role in a systematic restatement of our common knowledge about language. It is the detailed and parochial part – the part that would be different if we were Liars, or if we were Japanese. It attaches to the rest by way of the concept of truth-in-English (or in some other language), which the grammar supplies and which the rest of the restatement employs.

The subject might be differently delineated, and more stringent conditions of adequacy might be demanded. You might insist that a good grammar should be suited to fit into a psycholinguistic theory that goes beyond our common knowledge and explains the inner mechanisms that make our practice possible. There is nothing wrong in principle with this ambitious goal, but I doubt that it is worthwhile to pursue it in our present state of knowledge. Be that is it may, it is certainly not a goal I dare pursue.

3. CONTEXT-DEPENDENCE

Any adequate grammar must tell us that truth-in-English depends not only on what words are said and on the facts, but also on features of the situation in which the words are said. The dependence is surprisingly multifarious. If the words are 'Now I am hungry.' then some facts about who is hungry when matter, but also it matters when the speech occurs and who is speaking. If the words are 'France is hexagonal.' of course the shape of France matters, but so do the aspects of previous discourse that raise or lower the standards of precision. Truth-in-English has been achieved if the last thing said before was 'Italy is sort of boot-shaped.' but not if the last thing said before was 'Shapes in geometry are ever so much simpler than shapes in geography'. If the words are 'That one costs too much.' of course the prices of certain things matter, and it matters which things are traversed by the line projected from the speaker's pointing finger, but also the relations of comparative salience among these things matter. These relations in turn depend on various aspects of the situation, especially the previous discourse. If the words are 'Fred came floating up through the hatch of the spaceship and turned left.', then it matters what point of reference and what orientation we have established. Beware: these are established in a complicated way. (See Fillmore [3].) They need not be the location and orientation of the speaker, or of the audience, or of Fred, either now or at the time under discussion.

When truth-in-English depends on matters of fact, that is called *contingency*. When it depends on features of context, that is called *indexicality*. But need we distinguish? Some contingent facts are facts about context, but are there any that are not? Every context is located not only in physical space but also in logical space. It is at some particular possible world – our world if it is an actual context, another world if it is a merely possible context. (As you see, I presuppose a metaphysics of modal realism. It's not that I think this ontological commitment is indispensable to proper philosophy of language – in philosophy there are usually many ways to skin a cat. Rather, I reject the popular presumption that modal realism stands in need of justification.) It is a feature of any context, actual or otherwise, that its world is one where matters of contingent fact are a certain way. Just as truth-in-English may depend on the time of the context, or the speaker, or the standards of precision, or the salience relations, so likewise may it depend on the world of the context. Contingency is a kind of indexicality.

4. SEMANTIC VALUES

A concise grammar for a big language – for instance, a finite grammar for an infinite language like ours – had better work on the compositional principle. Most linguistic expressions must be built up stepwise, by concatenation or in some more complicated way, from a stock of basic expressions.

(Alternatively, structures that are not linguistic expressions may be built up stepwise, and some of these may be transformed into linguistic expressions. For evidence that these approaches differ only superficially, see Cooper and Parsons [4].)

To go beyond syntax, a compositional grammar must associate with each expression an entity that I shall call its *semantic value*. (In case of ambiguity, more than one must be assigned.) These play a twofold role. First, the semantic values of some expressions, the *sentences*, must enter somehow into determining whether truth-in-English would be achieved if the expression were uttered in a given context. Second, the semantic value of any expression is to be determined by the semantic values of the (immediate) constituents from which it is built, together with the way it is built from them.

To the extent that sentences are built up, directly or indirectly, from sentences, the semantic values of sentences have both jobs to do. The semantic values of non-sentences have only one job: to do their bit toward determining the semantic values of the sentences.

Semantic values may be anything, so long as their jobs get done. Different compositional grammars may assign different sorts of semantic values, yet succeed equally well in telling us the conditions of truth-in-English and therefore serve equally well as chapters in the systematic restatement of our common knowledge about language. Likewise, different but equally adequate grammars might parse sentences into different constituents, combined according to different rules.

More ambitious goals presumably would mean tighter constraints. Maybe a grammar that assigns one sort of semantic value could fit better into future psycholinguistics than one that assigns another sort. Thereof I shall not speculate.

Another source of obscure and unwanted constraints is our traditional semantic vocabulary. We have too many words for semantic values, and for the relation of having a semantic value:

apply to	express	represent
Bedeutung	extension	satisfy
character	fall under	sense
comply with	intension	signify
comprehension	interpretation	*Sinn*
concept	meaning	stand for
connotation	name	statement
denote	nominatum	symbolize
designate	refer	true of

for a start. Not just any of these words can be used for just any sort of assignment of semantic values, but it is far from clear which go with which. (See Lewis [9].) There are conflicting tendencies in past usage, and presuppositions we ought to abandon. So I have thought it best to use a newish and neutral term, thereby dodging all issues about which possible sorts of semantic values would deserve which of the familiar names.

5. SHIFTINESS

Often the truth (-in-English) of a sentence in a context depends on the truth of some related sentence when some feature of the original context is shifted. 'There have been dogs.' is true now iff 'There are dogs.' is true at some time before now. 'Somewhere the sun is shining.' is true here iff 'The sun is shining.' is true somewhere. 'Aunts must be women.' is true at our world iff 'Aunts are women.' is true at all worlds. 'Strictly speaking, France is not hexagonal.' is true even under low standards of precision iff 'France is not hexagonal.' is true under stricter standards.

In such a case, it may be good strategy for a compositional grammar to parse one sentence as the result of applying a modifier to another:

'There have been dogs.' = 'It has been that. . .' + 'There are dogs.'
'Somewhere the sun is shining.' = 'Somewhere. . .' + 'The sun is shining.'
'Aunts must be women.' = 'It must be that. . .' + 'Aunts are women.'
'Strictly speaking, France is not hexagonal.' = 'Strictly speaking. . .' + 'France is not hexagonal.'

Then if the semantic value of the first sentence is to determine its truth in various contexts, and if that value is to be determined by the values of constituents, then the value of the second sentence must provide information about how the second sentence varies in truth value when the relevant feature of context is shifted.

I emphasized that context-dependence was multifarious, but perhaps the shifty kind of context-dependence is less so. The list of shiftable features of context may be quite short. I have suggested that the list should include time, place, world, and (some aspects of) standards of precision. I am not sure what more should be added.

To be sure, we could speak a language in which 'As for you, I am hungry.' is true iff 'I am hungry.' is true when the role of speaker is shifted from me to you – in other words, iff you are hungry. We could – but we don't. For English, the speaker is not a shiftable feature of context. We could speak a language in which 'Backward, that one costs too much.' is true iff 'That one costs too much.' is true under a reversal of the direction the speaker's finger points. But we don't. We could speak a language in which 'Upside down, Fred came floating up through the hatch of the spaceship and turned left.' is true iff 'Fred came floating up through the hatch of the spaceship and turned left.' is true under a reversal of the orientation established in the original context. But we don't. There are ever so many conceivable forms of shiftiness that we don't indulge in.

(To forestall confusion, let me say that in calling a feature of context unshiftable, I do not mean that we cannot change it. I just mean that it does not figure in any rules relating truth of one sentence in context to truth of a second sentence when some feature of the original context is shifted. The established orientation of a context is changeable but probably not shiftable. The world of a context is shiftable but not changeable.)

We seem to have a happy coincidence. To do their first job of determining whether truth-in-English would be achieved if a given sentence were uttered in a given context, it seems that the semantic values of sentences must provide information about the dependence of truth on features of context. That seems to be the very information that is also needed, in view of shiftiness, if semantic values are to do their second job of helping to determine the semantic values of sentences with a given sentence as constituent. How nice.

No; we shall see that matters are more complicated.

6. CONTEXT AND INDEX

Whenever a sentence is said, it is said at some particular time, place, and world. The production of a token is located, both in physical space-time and in logical space. I call such a location a *context*.

That is not to say that the only features of context are time, place, and world. There are countless other features, but they do not vary independently. They are given by the intrinsic and relational character of the time, place, and world in question. The speaker of the context is the one who is speaking at that time, at that place, at that world. (There may be none; not every context is a context of utterance. I here ignore the possibility that more than one speaker might be speaking at the same time, place, and world.) The audience, the standards of precision, the salience relations, the presuppositions . . . of the context are given less directly. They are determined, so far as they are determined at all, by such things as the previous course of the conversation that is still going on at the context, the states of mind of the participants, and the conspicuous aspects of their surroundings.

Suppose a grammar assigns semantic values in such a way as to determine, for each context and each sentence (or for each disambiguation of each sentence), whether that sentence is true in that context. Is that enough? What more could we wish to know about the dependence of truth on features of context?

That is not enough. Unless our grammar explains away all seeming case of shiftiness, we need to know what happens to the truth values of constituent sentences when one feature of context is shifted and the rest are held fixed. But features of context do not vary independently. No two contexts differ by only one feature. Shift one feature only, and the result of the shift is not a context at all.

Example: under one disambiguation, 'If someone is speaking here then I exist.' is true at any context whatever. No shift from one context to another can make it false. But a time shift, holding other features fixed, can make it false; that is why 'Forevermore, if someone is speaking here then I will exist.' is false in the original context. Likewise a world shift can make it false; that is why 'Necessarily, if someone is speaking here then I must exist.' is false in the original context. The shifts that make the sentence false must not be shifts from one context to another.

The proper treatment of shiftiness requires not contexts but *indices*: packages of features of context so combined that they *can* vary independently. An index is an *n*-tuple of features of context of various sorts; call these features the *coordinates* of the index. We impose no requirement that the coordinates of an index should all be features of any one context. For instance, an index might have among its coordinates a speaker, a time before his birth, and a world where he never lived at all. Any *n*-tuple of things of the right kinds is an index. So, although we can never go from one context to another by shifting only one feature, we can always go from one index to another by shifting only one coordinate.

Given a context, there is an index having coordinates that match the appropriate features of that context. Call it the *index of* the context. If we start with the index of a context and shift one coordinate, often the result will be an index that is not the index of any context. That was the case for the time shifts and world shifts that made our example sentence 'If someone is speaking here then I exist.' go false.

Contexts have countless features. Not so for indices: they have the features of context that are packed into them as coordinates, and no others. Given an index, we cannot expect to recover the salience relations (for example) by asking what was salient to the speaker of the index at the time of the index at the world of the index. That method works for a context, or for the index of a context, but not for indices generally. What do we do if the speaker of the index does not exist at that time at that world? Or if the speaker never exists at that world? Or if the time does not exist at the world, since that world is one with circular time? The only way we can recover salience relations from an arbitrary index is if we have put them there as coordinates, varying independently of the other coordinates. Likewise for any other feature of context.

I emphasized that the dependence of truth on context was surprisingly multifarious. It would be no easy matter to devise a list of all the features of context that are sometimes relevant to truth-in-English. In [7] I gave a list that was long for its day, but not nearly long enough. Cresswell rightly complained:

> Writers who, like David Lewis, . . . try to give a bit more body to these notions talk about times, places, speakers, hearers, . . . etc. and then go through agonies of conscience in trying to decide whether they have taken account of enough. It seems to me impossible to lay down in advance what sort of thing is going to count [as a relevant feature of context]. . . . The moral here seems to be that there is no way of specifying a finite list of contextual coordinates. ([2], p. 8)

Cresswell goes on to employ objects which, though not the same as the time-place-world locations I have called contexts, are like them and unlike indices in giving information about indefinitely many features of context.

7. THE INDEXICALIST'S DILEMMA

To do their first job of determining whether truth-in-English would be achieved if a given sentence were uttered in a given context, the semantic values of sentences must provide information about the dependence of truth on context. Dependence on indices won't do, unless they are built inclusively enough to include every feature that is ever relevant to truth. We have almost certainly overlooked a great many features. So for the present, while the task of constructing an explicit grammar is still unfinished, the indices we know how to construct won't do. Indices are no substitute for contexts because contexts are rich in features and indices are poor.

To do their second job of helping to determine the semantic values of sentences with a given sentence as a constituent, the semantic values of sentences must provide information about the dependence of truth on indices. Dependence on contexts won't do, since we must look at the variation of truth value under shifts of one feature only. Contexts are no substitute for indices because contexts are not amenable to shifting.

Contexts and indices will not do each other's work. Therefore we need both. An adequate assignment of semantic values must capture two different dependencies of truth on features of context: context-dependence and index-dependence. We need the relation: sentence *s* is true at context *c* at index *i*. We need both the case in which *i* is the index of the context *c* and the case in which *i* has been shifted away, in one or more coordinates, from the index of the context. The former case can be abbreviated. Let us say that sentence *s* is true at context *c* iff *s* is true at *c* at the index of the context *c*.

Once we help ourselves to contexts and indices both, we need not go through agonies of conscience to make sure that no relevant features of context has been left out of the coordinates of our indices. Such difficult inclusiveness is needed only if indices are meant to replace contexts. If not, then it is enough to make sure that every shiftable feature of context is included as a coordinate. If most features of context that are relevant to truth are unshiftable, as it seems reasonable to hope, then it might not be too hard to list all the shiftable ones.

8. SCHMENTENCES

Besides the ambitious plan of dispensing with contexts after learning how to construct sufficiently inclusive indices, there is another way to evade my conclusion that we need context-dependence and index-dependence both. The latter was needed only for the treatment of shiftiness, and we might claim that there is no such thing. We can perfectly well build a compositional grammar in which it never happens that sentences are constituents of other sentences, or of anything else. (Make an exception if you like for truth-functional compounding, which isn't shifty; but I shall consider the strategy in its most extreme form.) In this grammar sentences are the output, but never an intermediate step, of the compositional process.

If we take this course, we will need replacements for the sentences hitherto regarded as constituents. The stand-ins will have to be more or less sentence-like. But we will no longer call them sentences, reserving that title for the output sentences. Let us call them *schmentences* instead. We can go on parsing 'There have been dogs.' as the result of applying 'It has been that. . .' to 'There are dogs.'; but we must now distinguish the constituent *schmentence* 'There are dogs.' from the homonymous *sentence*, which is not a constituent of anything. Now the semantic values of genuine sentences have only the first of their former jobs: determining whether truth-in-English would be achieved if a given sentence were uttered in a given context. For that job, dependence of truth on context is all we need. The second job, that of helping to determine the semantic values of sentences with a given constituent, now belongs to the semantic values of schmentences. That job, of course, still requires index-dependence (and context-dependence too, unless the indices are inclusive enough). But nothing requires index-dependent truth of genuine sentences. Instead of giving the semantic values of sentences what it takes to do a double job, we can divide the labour.

A variant of the schmentencite strategy is to distinguish schmentences from sentences syntactically. We might write the schmentences without a capital letter and a period. Or we might decorate the schmentences with free variables as appropriate. Then we might parse 'There have been dogs.' as the result of applying 'It has been that. . .' to the schmentence 'there are dogs at *t*' where '*t*' is regarded as a variable over times. The confusing homonymy between schmentences and sentences is thereby removed. Index-dependence of the schmentence thus derives from index-dependence of the values of its variables. Schmentences would be akin to the open formulas that figure in the standard treatment of quantification. Truth of a schmentence at an index would be like satisfaction of a formula by an assignment of values to variables. But while the schmentencite might proceed in this way, I insist that he need not. Not all is a variable that varies. If the coordinates of indices were homogeneous in kind and unlimited in number – which they are not – then it might be handy to use variables as a device for keeping track of exactly how the truth value of a schmentence depends on the various coordinates. But variables can be explained away even then (see Quine [14]); or rather, they can be replaced by other devices to serve the same purpose. If the coordinates of indices are few and different in kind, it is not clear that variables would even be a convenience.

(Just as we can liken index-dependent schmentences to formulas that depend for truth on the assignment of values to their free variables, so also we can go in the reverse direction. We can include the value assignments as coordinates of indices, as I did in [7], and thereby subsume assignment-dependence of formulas under index-dependence of sentences. However, this treatment is possible only if we limit the values of variables. For instance we cannot let a variable take as its value a function from indices, since that would mean that some index was a member of a member of. . . a member of itself – which is impossible.)

I concede this victory to the schmentencite: strictly speaking, we *do not need* to provide both context-dependence and index-dependence in the assignment of semantic values to geuine sentences. His victory is both cheap and pointless. I propose to ignore it.

9. DISTINCTION WITHOUT DIFFERENCE

Therefore, let us agree that sentences depend for their truth on both context and index. What, then, should we take as their semantic values? We have two options.

First option: the semantic values of sentences are *variable but simple*. A value for a sentence is a function, perhaps partial, from indices to truth values. (Alternatively, it is a set of indices.) However, a sentence may have different semantic values in different contexts, and the grammar must tell us how value depends on context. The grammar assigns a semantic value (or more than one, in case of ambiguity) to each sentence-context pair. The value in turn is something which, together with an index, yields a truth value. Diagrammatically:

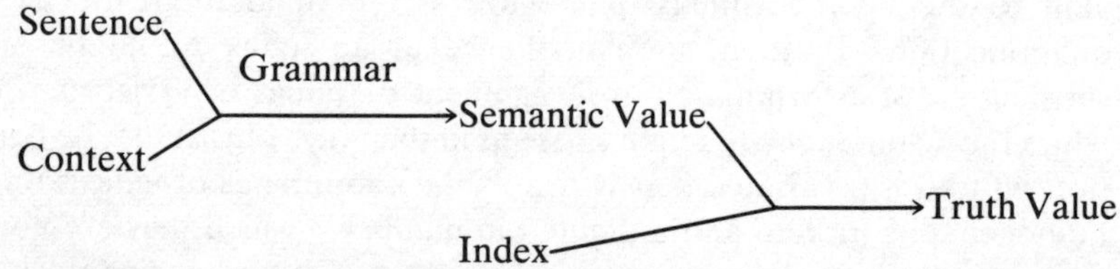

Sentence s is true at context c at index i iff $V^s_c(i)$ is truth, where V^s_c is the value of s at c. Sentence s is true at context c iff $V^s_c(i_c)$ is truth, where i_c is the index of the context c.

Second option: the semantic values of sentences are *constant but complicated*. A value for a sentence is a function, perhaps partial, from combinations of a context and an index to truth values. (Alternatively, it is a set of context-index combinations.) The semantic value of a sentence (or its set of values, in case of ambiguity) does not vary from context to context. The grammar assigns it once and for all. Diagrammatically:

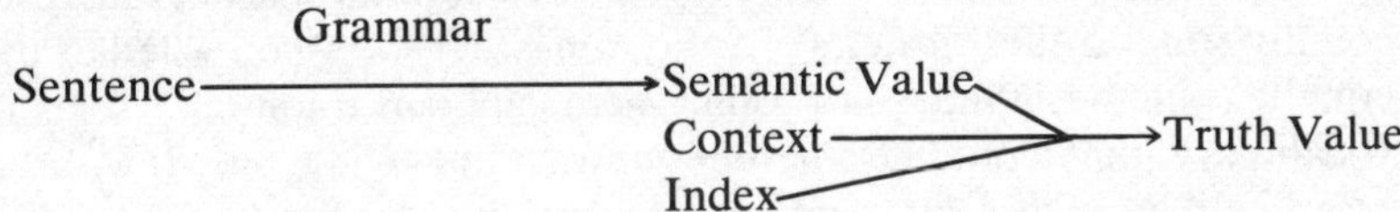

Sentence s is true at context c at index i iff $V^s(c + i)$ is truth, where V^s is the constant semantic value of s. Sentence s is true at context c iff $V^s(c + i_c)$ is truth, where i_c is the index of the context c. Context-index combinations could be taken in either of two ways: as pairs $\langle c, i\rangle$ of a context c and an index i, or alternatively as $(n + 1)$-tuples $\langle c, i_1, \ldots, i_n\rangle$ that start with c and continue with the n coordinates of i.

(It is worth mentioning and rejecting a zeroth option: the semantic values of sentences are *very variable but very simple*. They are simply truth values; however, a sentence has different semantic values at different context-index combinations. This option flouts the compositional principle, which requires that the semantic values of sentences be determined by the semantic values of their constituent sentences. The truth value of a sentence at a given context and index may depend not on the truth value of a constituent sentence at that context and index, but rather on its truth value at that context and other, shifted indices. The less I have said about what so-called semantic values must be, the more I am entitled to insist on what I *did* say. If they don't obey the compositional principle, they are not what I call semantic values.)

Asked to choose between our two options, you may well suspect that we have a distinction without a difference. Given a grammar that assigns semantic values according to one option, it is perfectly automatic to convert it into one of the other sort. Suppose given a grammar that assigns variable but simple semantic values: for any sentence s and context c, the value of s at c is V^s_c. Suppose you would prefer a grammar that assigns constant but complicated values. Very well: to each sentence s, assign once and for all the function V^s such that, for every context c and index i, $V^s(c + i)$ is $V^s_c(i)$. Or suppose given a grammar that assigns constant but complicated semantic values: to sentence s it assigns, once and for all, the value V^s. Suppose you would prefer a grammar that assigns variable but simple values. Very well: to the sentence s and context c, assign the function V^s_c such that, for every index i, $V^s_c(i)$ is $V^s(c + i)$.

Given the ease of conversion, how could anything of importance possibly turn on the choice betwen our two options? Whichever sort of assignment we are given, we have the other as well; and the assigned entities equally well deserve the name of semantic values because they equally well do the jobs of semantic values. (If we asked whether they equally well deserved some other name in our traditional semantic vocabulary, that would be a harder question but an idle one. If we asked whether they would fit equally well into future psycholinguistics, that would – in my opinion – be a question so hard and speculative as to be altogether futile.) How could the choice between the options possibly be a serious issue?

I have certainly not taken the issue very seriously. In [7] I opted for constant but complicated semantic values (though not quite as I described them here, since I underestimated the agonies of constructing sufficiently rich indices). But in [6] and [8], written at about the same time, I thought it made for smoother exposition to use variable but simple values (again, not quite as described here). I thought the choice a matter of indifference, and took for granted that my readers would think so to.

But I was wrong. Robert Stalnaker [11] and David Kaplan [5] have taken the issue very seriously indeed. They have argued that we ought to prefer the first option: variable but simple semantic values. Each thinks that simple, context-dependent semantic values of the proper sort (but not complicated constant ones) are good because they can do an extra job, besides the two jobs for semantic values that we have been considering so far. They differ about what this extra job is, however, and accordingly they advocate somewhat different choices of variable but simple values.

10. CONTENT AS OBJECT OF ATTITUDES: STALNAKER

In Stalnaker's theory, the semantic value of a sentence in context (after disambiguation) is a *proposition*: a function from possible worlds to truth values. Diagrammatically:

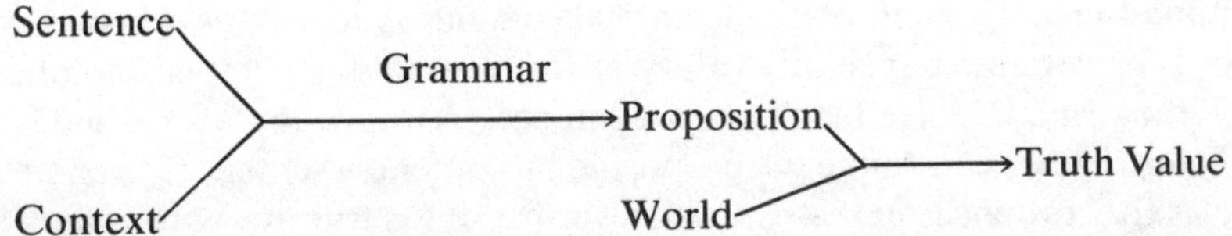

He mentions the alternative analysis on which a sentence is assigned, once and for all, a function from context-world combinations to truth values.

> It is a simpler analysis than the one I am sketching; I need some argument for the necessity or desirability of the extra step on the road from sentences to truth values. This step is justified only if the middlemen – the propositions – are of some independent interest, ... The independent interest in propositions comes from the fact that they are the objects of illocutionary acts and propositional attitudes. A proposition is supposed to be the common content of statements, judgements, promises, wishes and wants, questions and answers, things that are possible or probable. ([11], pp. 277–278)

I agree with much of this. Stalnaker is right that we can assign propositional content to sentences in context, taking propositions as functions from worlds to truth values. He is also right that propositions have an independent interest as suitable objects for attitudes such as belief, and in the other ways he mentions. (Here I pass over a big idealization; it could be defended in several ways and I am not sure which I prefer.) Furthermore, an account of truthful communication – not part of the grammar itself, but another chapter in the systematic restatement of our common knowledge about language – must concern itself at least implicitly with the relations between the propositional objects of the speaker's attitudes and the propositional content of his sentences.

To revert to our initial example: I know, and you need to know, whether *A* or *B* or . . .; so I say a sentence that I take to be true-in-English, in its context, and that depends for its truth on whether *A* or *B* or . . .; and thereby, if all goes well, you find out what you needed to know. My choice of what to say is guided by my beliefs. It depends on whether I believe the proposition true at exactly the *A*-worlds, or the one true at exactly the *B*-worlds, or . . . . In the simplest case, the sentence I choose to say is one whose propositional content (in English, in context) is whichever one of these propositions I believe.

That is all very well, but it does not mean that we need to equate the propositional content and the semantic value of a sentence in context. It is enough that the assignment of semantic values should somehow determine the assignment of propositional content. And it does, whether we opt for variable but simple values or for constant but complicated ones. Either way, we have the relation: sentence s is true at context c at index i. From that we can define the propositional content of sentence s in context c as that proposition that is true at world e iff s is true at c at the index i_c^w that results if we take the index i_c of the context c and shift its world coordinate to w.

(We can call this the *horizontal propositional content* of s in c; borrowing and modifying a suggestion of Stalnaker in [12] we could also define the *diagonal propositional content* of s in c. Suppose someone utters s in c but without knowing whether the context of his utterance is c or whether it is some other possible context in some other world which is indistinguishable from c. Since all ignorance about contingent matters of fact is ignorance about features of context, the sort of ignorance under consideration is a universal predicament. Let c^w be that context, if there is one, that is located at world w and indistinguishable from c; then for all the speaker knows he might inhabit w and c^w might be the context of his utterance. (I ignore the case of two indistinguishable contexts at the same world.) Let i_{c^w} be the index of the context c^w; note that this may differ from the index i_c^w mentioned above, since the contexts c and c_w will differ not only in world but in other features as well and the indices of the differing contexts may inherit some of their differences. We define the diagonal content of s in c as that proposition that is true at a world w iff (1) there is a context c^w of the sort just considered, and (2) s is true at c^w at i_{c^w}. Stalnaker shows in [12] that horizontal and diagonal content both enter into an account of linguistic communication. The former plays the central role if there is no significant ignorance of features of context relevant to truth; otherwise we do well to consider the latter instead. Stalnaker speaks of reinterpreting sentences in certain contexts so that they express their diagonal rather than their horizontal content. I find this an inadvisable way of putting the point, since if there is a horizontal-diagonal ambiguity it is very unlike ordinary sorts of ambiguity. I doubt that we can perceive it as an ambiguity; it is neither syntactic nor lexical; and it is remarkably widespread. I think it might be better to say that a sentence in context has both a horizontal and a diagonal content; that these may or may not be the same; and that they enter in different ways into an account of communication. Be that as it may, I shall from now on confine my attention to propositional content of the horizontal sort; but what I say would go for diagonal content also.)

It would be a convenience, nothing more, if we could take the propositional content of a sentence in context as its semantic value. But we cannot. The propositional contents of sentences do not obey the compositional principle, therefore they are not semantic values. Such are the ways of shiftiness that the propositional content of 'Somewhere the sun is shining.' in context *c* is not determined by the content in *c* of the constituent sentence 'The sun is shining.'. For an adequate treatment of shiftiness we need not just world-dependence but index-dependence – dependence of truth on all the shiftable features of context. World is not the only shiftable feature.

(Stalnaker does suggest, at one point, that he might put world-time pairs in place of worlds. "Does a tensed sentence determine a proposition which is sometimes true, sometimes false, or does it express different timeless propositions at different times? I doubt that a single general answer can be given." ([11], p. 289) But this does not go far enough. World and time are not the only shiftable features of context. And also perhaps it goes too far. If propositions are reconstrued so that they may vary in truth from one time to another, are they still suitable objects for propositional attitudes?)

There is always the schmentencite way out: to rescue a generalization, reclassify the exceptions. If we said that the seeming sentences involved in shiftiness of features other than world (and perhaps time) were not genuine sentences, then we would be free to say that the semantic value of a genuine sentence, in context, was its propositional content. But what's the point?

I have been a bit unfair to complain that the propositional content of a sentence in context is not its semantic value. Stalnaker never said it was. 'Semantic value' is my term, not his. Nor did he falsely claim that contents obeys the compositional principle.

But my point can be stated fairly. Nothing is wrong with what Stalnaker says, but by omission he gives a misleading impression of simplicity. Besides the propositional content of a given sentence in a given context, and besides the function that yields the content of a given sentence in any context, we need something more – something that goes unmentioned in Stalnaker's theory. We need an assignment of semantic values to sentences (or to schmentences) that captures the dependence of truth both on context and on index, and that obeys the compositional principle. An assignment of variable but simple semantic values would meet the need, and so would an assignment of constant but complicated ones.

Neither of these could *be* the assignment of propositional content. Either would suffice to determine it. So Stalnaker's discussion of propositional content affords no reason for us to prefer variable but simple semantic values rather than constant but complicated ones.

11. CONTENT AS WHAT IS SAID: KAPLAN

Kaplan [5], unlike Stalnaker, clearly advocates the assignment of variable but simple semantic values as I have described it here. His terminology is like Stalnaker's, but what he calls the content of a sentence in context is a function from moderately rich indices to truth values. Diagrammatically:

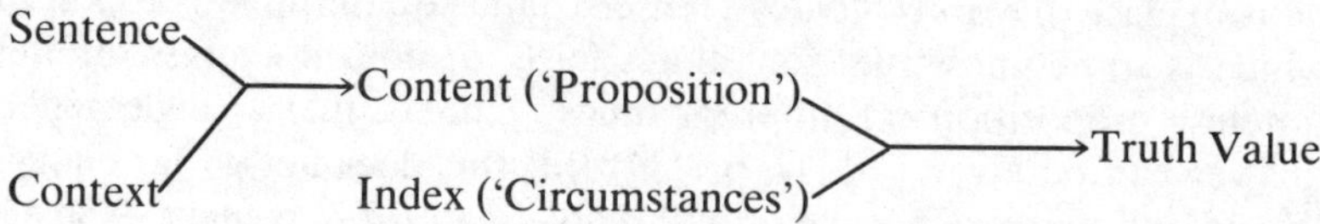

I cannot complain against Kaplan, as I did against Stalnaker, that his so-called contents are not semantic values because they violate compositionality. But Kaplan cannot plausibly claim, as Stalnaker did, that his contents have an independent interest as suitable objects for propositional attitudes.

Kaplan claims a different sort of independent interest for his contents – that is, for variable but simple semantic values. We have the intuitive, pre-theoretical notion of 'what is said' by a sentence in context. We have two sentences in two contexts, or one sentence in two contexts, or two sentences in one context; and we judge that what has been said is or is not the same for both sentence-context pairs. Kaplan thinks that if we assign simple, context-dependent semantic values of the right sort, then we can use them to explicate our judgements of sameness of what is said: what is said by sentence s_1 in context c_1 is the same as what is said by sentence s_2 in context c_2 iff the semantic value of s_1 in c_1 and the semantic value of s_2 in c_2 are identical. Indeed, Kaplan suggests that our informal locution 'what is said' is just a handy synonym for his technical term 'content'.

> Thus if I say, today,. 'I was insulted yesterday.' and you utter the same words tomorrow what is said is different. If what we say differs in truth value, that is enough to show that we say different things. But even if the truth values were the same, it is clear that there are possible circumstances in which what I said would be true but what you said would be false. Thus we say different things. Let us call this first kind of meaning – what is said – *content*. ([5], p. 19)

Consider some further examples. (1) I say 'I am hungry.'. You simultaneously say to me 'You are hungry.'. What is said is the same. (2) I say 'I am hungry.'. You simultaneously say 'I am hungry.'. What is said is not the same. Perhaps what I said is true but what you said isn't. (3) I say on 6 June 1977 'Today is Monday.'. You say on 7 June 1977 'Yesterday was Monday.'. What is said is the same. (4) Same for me, but you say on 7 June 1977 'Today is Tuesday.'. What is said is the same. (5) I say on 6 June 1977 'It is Monday.'. I might have said, in the very same context, '6 June 1977 is Monday.'. or perhaps 'Today is Monday.'. What is said is not the same. What I did say is false on six days out of every seven, whereas the two things I might have said are never false.

I put it to you that not one of these examples carries conviction. In every case, the proper naive response is that in some sense what is said is the same for both sentence-context pairs, whereas in another – equally legitimate – sense, what is said is not the same. Unless we give it some special technical meaning, the locution 'what is said' is very far from univocal. It can mean the propositional content, in Stalnaker's sense (horizontal or diagonal). It can mean the exact words. I suspect that it can mean almost anything in between. True, what is said is the same, in some sense, iff the semantic value is the same according to a grammar that assigns variable but simple values. So what, unless the sense in question is more than one among many? I think it is also so that what is said is the same, in some sense, iff the semantic value is the same according to a grammar that assigns constant but complicated values.

Kaplan's readers learn to focus on the sense of 'what is said' that he has in mind, ignoring the fact that the same words can be used to make different distinctions. For the time being, the words mark a definite distinction. But why mark that distinction rather than others that we could equally well attend to? It is not a special advantage of variable but simple semantic values that they can easily be used to explicate those distinctions that they can easily be used to explicate.

12. SOLIDARITY FOREVER

I see Stalnaker and Kaplan as putting forth package deals. Offered the whole of either package – take it or leave it – I take it. But I would rather divide the issues. Part of each package is a preference, which I oppose as unwarranted and arbitrary, for variable but simple semantic values. But there is much in each package that I applaud; and that I have incorporated into the proposals of the present paper, whichever option is chosen. In particular there are three points on which Stalnaker and Kaplan and I join in disagreeing with my earlier self, the author of [7].

First, the author of [7] thought it an easy thing to construct indices richly enough to include all features of context that are ever relevant to truth. Stalnaker and Kaplan and I all have recourse to genuine context-dependence and thereby shirk the quest for rich indices. Stalnaker and Kaplan do not dwell on this as a virtue of their theories, but it is one all the same.

Second, I take it that Stalnaker and Kaplan and I join in opposing any proposal for constant but complicated but not complicated enough semantic values that would ignore the following distinction. There are sentences that are true in any context, but perhaps not necessarily true; and there are sentences in context that are necessarily true, though perhaps the same sentence is not necessarily true, or not true at all, in another context. (This is at least an aspect of Kripke's well-known distinction between the *a priori* and the necessary.) The distinction might be missed by a treatment that simply assigns functions from indices to truth values (as in [7]), or functions from contexts to truth values, as the constant semantic values of sentences. It is captured by any treatment that combines context-dependence and index-dependence, as in Kaplan's theory or the treatment proposed here; it is likewise captured by any treatment that combines context-dependence and world-dependence, as in Stalnaker's theory or my [6] and [8]. In the first case it is the distinction between (1) a sentence that is true at every context c at the index i_c of c, and (2) a sentence that is true at a particular context c at every index i_c^w that comes from the index i_c of the context c by shifting the world coordinate. In the second case it is the distinction between (1) a sentence that is true at every context c at the world of c, and (2) a sentence that is true at some particular context c at every world.

Third, all three of us, unlike the author of [7], have availed ourselves of the device of *double indexing*. Context-dependence and index-dependence (or world-dependence) together give a double world-dependence: truth may depend both on the world of the context and on the world-coordinate of the index, and these may differ since the latter may have been shifted That facilitates the semantic analysis of such modifiers as 'actually': 'Actually ϕ.' is true at context c at index i iff ϕ is true at c at i^w, the index that comes from i by shifting the world coordinate to the world w of the context c. Similarly, context-dependence and index-dependence together give a double time-dependence (if indices have time coordinates) so that we can give a version of Kamp's analysis of 'now': 'Now ϕ.' is true at context c at index i iff ϕ is true at c at i^t, the index that comes from i by shifting the time coordinate to the time t of the context c.

For extensive discussions of the uses and origins of double indexing, see Kaplan [5] and van Fraassen [13]. However, there is a measure of disappointment in store. For some uses of double indexing, it is enough to have double world-dependence (or time-dependence) in which the world (or time) appears once shiftably and once unshiftably. 'Actually' (or 'now'), for instance, will always bring us back to the world (or time) of the context. For these uses, the extra world-dependence and time-dependence that come as part of context-dependence will meet our needs. But there are other applications of double indexing, no less useful in the semanticist's toolbox, that require double shiftability. The principal application in [13] is of this sort. Moreover, if we combine several applications that each require double shiftability, we may then need more than double indexing. Coordinates that have been shifted for one purpose are not available unshifted for another purpose. If we want multiply shiftable multiple indexing, then we will have to repeat the world or time coordinates of our indices as many times over as needed. The unshiftable world and time of the context will take us only part of the way.

ACKNOWLEDGEMENTS

I am grateful to many friends for valuable discussions of the material in this paper. Special mention is due to Max Cresswell, Gareth Evans, Charles Fillmore, David Kaplan, and Robert Stalnaker. An early version was presented to the Vacation School in Logic at Victoria University of Wellington in August 1976; I thank the New Zealand–United States Educational Foundation for research support on that occasion.

BIBLIOGRAPHY

[1] Yehoshua Bar-Hillel, 'Indexical Expressions', *Mind* **63** (1954), 359–379.

[2] M. J. Cresswell, 'The World is Everything That is The Case', *Australasian Journal of Philosophy* **50** (1972), 1–13.

[3] Charles Fillmore, 'How to Know Whether You're Coming or Going', in *Studies in Descriptive and Applied Linguistics: Bulletin of the Summer Institute in Linguistics V* (International Christian University, Tokyo).

[4] Robin Cooper and Terence Parsons, 'Montague Grammar, Generative Semantics and Interpretive Semantics', in Barbara Partee (ed.), *Montague Grammar* (Academic Press, 1976).

[5] David Kaplan, 'Demonstratives', presented at the 1977 meeting of the Pacific Division of the American Philosophical Association. (Precursors of this paper, with various titles, have circulated widely since about 1971.)

[6] David Lewis, *Convention: A Philosophical Study* (Harvard University Press, 1969).

[7] David Lewis, 'General Semantics', *Synthese* **22** (1970), 18–67; and in Barbara Partee (ed.), *Montague Grammar* (Academic Press, 1976).

[8] David Lewis, 'Languages and Language', in *Minnesota Studies in the Philosophy of Science*, Vol. VII (University of Minnesota Press, 1975).

[9] David Lewis, ''Tensions', in Milton Munitz and Peter Unger (eds.), *Semantics and Philosophy* (New York University Press, 1974).

[10] Richard Montague, 'Pragmatics', in Montague, *Formal Philosophy* (Yale University Press, 1974).

[11] Robert Stalnaker, 'Pragmatics', *Synthese* **22** (1970), 272–289.

[12] Robert Stalnaker, 'Assertion', in Peter Cole (ed.), *Syntax and Semantics 9* (New York, 1978).

[13] Bas van Fraassen, 'The Only Necessity is Verbal Necessity', *Journal of Philosophy* **74** (1977), 71–85.

[14] W. V. Quine, 'Variables Explained Away', in Quine, *Selected Logic Papers* (Random House, 1966).

JAMES D. McCAWLEY

FUZZY LOGIC AND RESTRICTED QUANTIFIERS*

This paper is part of an ongoing attempt to do justice to both a linguist's concerns and a logician's within a single consistent system. The principal respect in which a linguist's concerns will affect what follows here is the matter of coverage: I will assume Lakoff's (1972) conclusion that a multi-valued logic is essential for an adequate treatment of the semantics of a large amount of natural language vocabulary, particularly adjectives such as *fat*, *obnoxious*, and *pleasant*, which do not make a clear division between things of which they are true and things of which they are false, nouns such as *vermin*, *vegetable*, and *toy*, which denote categories with imprecise boundaries, and many 'hedge' words such as *somewhat, quite, pretty much,* and *par excellence*. I will take truth values to be real numbers on the interval from 0 to 1, with 0 corresponding to unqualified falsehood, 1 to unqualified truth, and intermediate numbers to intermediate degrees of truth to which such terms as 'fairly true', 'pretty well false', and the like could be applied[1].

I am particularly interested in versions of fuzzy logic which turn out to include classical logic as a special case, i.e. versions of fuzzy logic whose truth conditions for the various connectives reduce to the classical truth tables when the truth values of atomic propositions are restricted to 0 and 1, and whose rules of inference reduce to 'classical rules' when distinctions relevant only to non-classical truth values are ignored. That is, I cherish the hope that a logic which is adequate for the semantic diversity actually present in natural language will be what I would call an 'extension' of classical logic if it weren't that a recent book (Haack 1975) has used the term 'extension' in a different sense. Haack speaks of one logic being an 'extension' when the set of its well-formed formulas contains the set of wff's of the other logic, and the valid formulas (or the theorems) of the smaller logic are valid (or are theorems) in the 'extension'. The system of fuzzy logic that I will be exploring below will be an 'extension' of classical predicate logic in the sense that you get classical logic if you ignore the non-classical truth values. However, it will not be an 'extension' in Haack's sense, since not all classically valid formulas will be valid in it: there will be many formulas which take on only the value 1

S. Kanger and S. Öhman (eds.), Philosophy and Grammar, 101–118.

when their atomic constituents have classical truth values but can take on lower truth values when their atomic constituents have values other than 0 and 1.[2]

I will also be interested in determining to what extent a system of rules of 'natural deduction' for classical logic can be retained even within the more general fuzzy system. In investigating this question, I will impose a fairly stringent condition as to when a system of truth value assignment and a system of rules of inference can be said to 'fit'. I wish to require more than merely that when applied to true premises, the rules of inference must yield true conclusions. That condition, of course, does not distinguish among different truth values that are less than 1. I propose instead to generalize this last condition to the condition that in any inference that conforms to the given rules, the conclusion cannot be less true than the 'weakest' premise, i.e. if $\{A_1, A_2, \ldots, A_n\} \vdash B$, then $/B/ \geq \min\,(/A_1/, /A_2/, \ldots, /A_n/)$. According to this criterion of 'fit', a system of valuations 'fits' a system of rules of inference if the rules of inference never 'reduce truth values': if they yield a conclusion of low truth value, there must have been a premise with truth vaue at least as low.

I will concentrate on the version of fuzzy propositional logic in which the propositional connectives are truth-functional[3] and have the following truth conditions:

(1) (a) $/{\sim}A/ = 1 - /A/$
(b) $/{\vee}AB/ = \max\,(/A/, /B/)$
(c) $/{\wedge}AB/ = \min\,(/A/, /B/)$
(d) $/{\supset}AB/ = 1 \quad \text{if} \quad /A/ \leq /B/$
$\qquad\qquad\quad /B/ \quad \text{if} \quad /A/ > /B/$

The truth conditions for $\sim$, $\wedge$, and $\vee$ are the natural generalizations of Łukasiewicz's 3-valued truth tables to the case of arbitrary truth values on the interval from 0 to 1. The truth conditions for the conditional are the same as in the system proposed by Gödel (summarized in Rescher 1969, 44). I accept the Gödel truth condition for the conditional, rather than the Łukasiewicz conditions, since the Gödel conditions fit the rule of modus ponens whereas the Łukasiewicz conditions do not: the Gödel conditions ensure that $/B/$ cannot be less than both $/A/$ and $/{\supset}AB/$. Indeed, the Gödel conditions can be said to preserve a popular rationale for the classical truth table for the conditional, namely that they make a conditional proposition as true as it can possibly bc and still not conflict with modus ponens.

Note that only some classically valid formulas will be valid in this system:

(2)

Valid	Invalid
$\supset AA$	$\vee(A, \sim A)$
$\supset(A, \supset BA)$	$\sim\wedge(A, \sim A)$
$\supset(\sim\wedge AB, \vee(\sim A, <B))$ and the other de Morgan laws	$\supset(\wedge(A, \sim A), B)$
$\vee(\supset AB, \supset BA)$	$\supset(B, \vee(A, \sim A))$
Commutative, associative, and idempotent laws for $\wedge$ and $\vee$.	$\supset(\supset AB, \supset(\sim B, \sim A))$
$\supset(\sim\supset AB, \sim B)$	$\supset(\wedge(\vee AB, \sim B), A)$
	$\supset(\supset AB, \vee(\sim A, B))$
	$\supset(\vee(\sim A, B), \supset AB)$
	$\supset(\sim\supset AB, A)$

To the extent that this system is the 'right logic' for discussing the semantics of natural language, it supports the negative visceral reaction that I have always had to the popular definition of $\vee$ in terms of $\supset$ and $\sim$, or of $\supset$ in terms of $\vee$ and $\sim$: while those 'definitions' give the right truth values in the classical case, the truth values of the definiens and definiendum can diverge when non-classical truth values are involved.

The system of natural deduction for classical propositional logic that I will take as a starting point consists of the 9 rules of inference in (3). Vertical lines here mark off subproofs, with horizontal lines separating the supposition of a subproof from the remainder of the subproof. Each rule is taken as justifying any step in which the formula derived has the indicated form and the formulas and subproofs from which it is inferred occur earlier than it (though not necessarily as consecutive steps nor in the given order) and either superordinate to it or in the same subproof as it. 'Reiteration' thus justifies repeating any superordinate step of the proof.

(3)

$\wedge$-introduction	$\vee$-introduction	$\supset$-introduction	$\sim$-introduction	reiteration
A	A B		A		A	
B	$\vee AB$ $\vee AB$		———		———	
$\wedge AB$			. . .		. . .	
			B		B	
		$\supset AB$		$\sim B$	A
			$\sim A$	A

∧-exploitation[4]	∨-exploitation	⊃-exploitation (= modus ponens)	~-exploitation
∧*AB* ∧*AB* *A* *B*	∨*AB* | *A* | . . . | *C* | *B* | . . . | *C* *C*	⊃*AB* *A* *B*	~~*A* *A*

It can readily be established that seven of these rules (namely, all but ~-introduction and reiteration) fit the truth conditions (1). Proving this in the case of ∨-elimination and ⊃-introduction (see Appendix A) involves showing that if a conclusion derived by the rule in question has a truth value lower than all operative premises, then the blame for that condition can be shifted onto earlier steps in the proof: at some point earlier in the proof a formula will have been derived whose truth value is less than that of all the premises that are operative at that point in the proof.

It is easy to find proofs in which a combination of ~-introduction and reiteration yield a conclusion of lower truth values than any of the premises:

(4)

			truth value
1	*B*	premise	0.5
2	~*B*	premise	0.5
3	| *A*	supposition	1
4	| *B*	1, reit	
5	| ~*B*	2, reit	
6	~*A*	3–5, ~-intro	0

Here a conclusion of truth value 0 is inferred from premises of truth value 0.5. How exactly to revise the rules (3) to bring them into fit with the truth conditions (1) is not obvious, though I conjecture that something close to the 'relevant entailment logic' of Chapter 4 of Anderson and Belnap (1975) will provide the desired fit. In place of the single rule of

~-introduction of (3), Anderson and Belnap have the following two rules:

(5) (a)

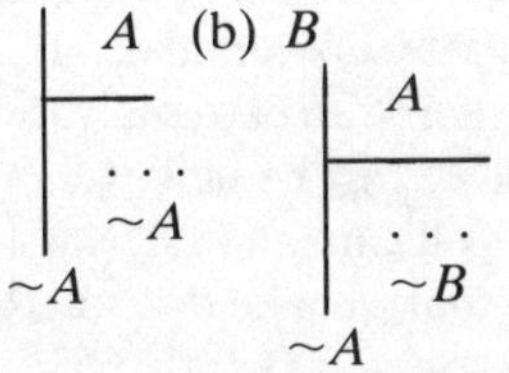

$$\begin{array}{l|l} & A \\ \cline{2-2} & \ldots \\ & {\sim}A \\ \multicolumn{2}{l}{{\sim}A} \end{array}$$

(b)

$$\begin{array}{l} B \\ \begin{array}{l|l} & A \\ \cline{2-2} & \ldots \\ & {\sim}B \end{array} \\ {\sim}A \end{array}$$

In addition, they index suppositions, keep track of the suppositions used in deriving each line, and allow subproofs only when the supposition of the subproof is used in deriving the conclusion of that subproof (thus disallowing such subproofs as 3–5 in (4), in which the supposition does not figure in the justification of lines 4 and 5). (5a) clearly does not fit the truth conditions (1), since it allows one to prove the theorem $\supset(\supset(A,{\sim}A),{\sim}A)$, but that formula takes the truth value $1 - /A/$ if $/A/ < 0.5$. Otherwise, Anderson and Belnap's rules fit (1). However, I am not yet clear as to what the implications of dropping (5a) from Anderson and Belnap's system are.

With an apology for leaving unsettled the question of how, if at all, the truth conditions (1) can be made to fit a system of rules of inference, I turn now to the question that will occupy me for the remainder of this paper, namely that of how to fit quantification into the system of fuzzy truth conditions that I have just sketched. Lakoff (1972) proposes the following truth conditions for quantifiers in fuzzy logic:[5]

(6) $/(\forall x)fx/ = \min_x /fx/$
$/(\exists x)fx/ = \max_x /fx/$

Lakoff here assumes a system of UNRESTRICTED QUANTIFIERS, in which every bound variable has the entire universe of discourse as its domain, and the effect of a restriction on the domain is simulated by applying a universal quantifier to a conditional expression and the existential quantifier to a conjoined expression, as in the popular analyses of (7a–b) as (8a–b):

(7) (a) All philosophers are dangerous.
(b) Some linguists are insane.

(8) (a) $(\forall x)\supset$(Philosopher x, Dangerous x)
(b) $(\exists x)\wedge$(Linguist x, Insane x)

Suppose that we accept these analyses and see what truth conditions we get when the constituent predicates are fuzzy, assuming the truth conditions (1) and (6).[6] *All fat persons are jolly* would be assigned as its truth value the minimum value that $\supset$(fat x, jolly x) ever takes.[7] But that means that *All fat persons are jolly* will get assigned an extremely low truth value for irrelevant reasons. By taking /jolly x/ to be as low as you like and taking /fat x/ to be anything greater, you can make /$\supset$(fat x, jolly x)/ as low as you like. In particular, suppose that we take /Nelson Rockefeller is fat/ = 0.3 and /Nelson Rockefeller is jolly/ = 0.2; then the existence of Nelson Rockefeller means that *All fat persons are jolly* can have at most the truth value 0.2. But that is absurd. Nelson Rockefeller is at best an extremely weak counterexample to the proposition that all fat persons are jolly. More importantly, under Lakoff's proposal for the truth conditions for quantifiers, an extremely weak counterexample such as Nelson Rockefeller would make just as big a dent in the truth value of *All fat persons are jolly* as would a really serious counterexample. I would assign to 'Marlon Brando is fat' a truth value of 0.9 or higher, and to 'Marlon Brando is jolly' a truth value of about 0.2. Brando is then a serious counterexample to the proposition that all fat persons are jolly; however, Brando and Rockefeller would make exactly the same contribution to the truth value of *All fat persons are jolly*: they would both impose an upper bound of 0.2 on the truth value of the general proposition.

While I won't have anything particularly to say about modal logic in this paper, I will take this opportunity to remark that the problem of the last paragraph also arises in the case of fuzzy modal logic. Suppose that we treat truth conditions for modal logic in terms of possible worlds linked by an alternativeness relation, as in Kripke (1959, 1963), but allow the alternativeness relation to be a 'fuzzy relation', i.e. allow Rww' to have truth values between 0 and 1. This gives a notion of 'alternative world' that is very like that of Lewis' (1974) analysis of counterfactuals, though not exactly the same notion, since I allow for /Rww'/ = 1 even when $w' \neq w$, whereas for Lewis any two distinct worlds are always 'some distance apart'. I do not intend that the degree to which w' is an alternative world to w should be a measure of the similarity of w' to w. It might be, say, a measure of how much in the way of a difference in the history that led up to w would result in w' rather than w being the 'present world', allowing for the fact that a minor change in the past (such as better aim on the part of an assassin) can result in major differences in the present. The truth value of $\Box A$ in a given world w might as a first approximation be taken to be the minimum truth value of A in the worlds w' that are alternatives to w. But how much of an alternative to w does a world w' have to be for a low truth value of A in w' to force a low truth value on $\Box A$ in w? Suppose, for example, that in all worlds that are unqualified alternatives to the real world, the truth value of *Chomsky is a genius* is 1, but in some world which is only weakly alternative to the real world, /Chomsky is a genius/ = 0.2. Should that mean that /Necessarily Chomsky is a genius/ in the real world must be 0.2 or less? If not, then we have essentially the same problem as with the status of Nelson Rockefeller as a counterexample to the proposition that all fat persons are jolly.

If plausible truth values are to be assigned to universal propositions involving fuzzy predicates, then the truth conditions for the universal quantifier will have to be revised so as to conform to the idea that an individual should be able to reduce the truth value of a universal proposition only in proportion to the extent to which he is a counterexample to it, and the measure of counterexamplehood will have to reflect the idea that an individual is not a serious counterexample to 'All f's are g's' unless he is an f to at least a fair extent. Suppose that at least as a makeshift we adopt the following measure of counterexamplehood: an individual is a counterexample to 'All f's are g's' to an extent given by the degree to which he is an f, multiplied by the amount by which his f-ness exceeds his g-ness: $/fx/(/fx/ - /gx/)$. Note that this satisfies the most obvious constraint on counterexamplehood: its maximum value is 1, which it attains when $/fx/ = 1$ and $/gx/ = 0$, the case of a counterexample par excellence. It is lower for individuals whose f-ness is lower and whose f-ness exceeds their g-ness by less. This measure of counterexamplehood would correspond to the following truth conditions for a universal quantifier:

$$\text{(9)} \qquad \begin{aligned} /(\forall x{:}fx)gx/ &= 1 - \max_x /fx/(/fx/ - /gx/) \\ &= \min_x(1 - /fx/(/fx/ - /gx/)) \end{aligned}$$

I have given (9) in terms of restricted rather than unrestricted quantification, since there is no apparent way in which an account in terms of unrestricted quantification could be reconciled with (9); in particular, it could not very well be regarded as a combination of (6) with some new proposal for the truth conditions of a conditional, since if $1 - /A/(/A/ - /B/)$ were the truth value of $\supset AB$, modus ponens could lead to conclusions weaker than the premises, e.g.

(10) $\supset AB$ 0.86
A 0.7
B 0.5

According to the measure of counterexamplehood embodied in (9), Rockefeller and Brando make reasonable contributions to the truth value of *All fat persons are jolly*: Brando would be a counterexample to extent 0.63, whereas Rockefeller would be a counterexample only to extent 0.03, i.e. the existence of someone like Brando would mean that *All fat persons are jolly* could have at most the truth value 0.37, whereas the existence of someone like Rockefeller would be consistent with its having the truth value 0.97.

(9) has the desired property that it includes the classical truth conditions as a special case: if $/fx/$ and $/gx/$ can only take on the values 0 and 1, then the universal proposition will be false if there is a counterexample (i.e. an instance in which $/fx/ = 1$ and $/gx/ = 0$) and will be true otherwise.

Let us now turn to the existential quantifier. If we want the truth conditions for existential propositions and for universal propositions to remain connected by the de Morgan laws (i.e. if the truth value of *All fat persons are jolly* is to be the same as that of *There isn't any fat person who isn't jolly*), then the truth conditions for the existential quantifier will also have to be something other than what is given by (6). Specifically, $\max_x /fx/(/fx/ - /gx/)$ would have to be the truth value of *Some fat person is not jolly*, and by replacing gx by $\sim gx$, we would get that the truth value of 'Some f's are g's' is given by:

(11) $/(\exists x{:}fx)gx/ = \max_x /fx/(/fx/ + /gx/ - 1)$

This formula has a similar advantage over (6) to what we found in the universal case: it allows examples to affect the truth value of the quantified proposition in proportion to their relevance to it, in cases where Lakoff's treatment would cause examples of different relevance to make the same contribution. For example, suppose that we have individuals as follows:

(12)

	/tall x/	/obnoxious x/
Sam	0.9	0.6
Jack	0.6	0.6
Fred	0.6	0.9

In each case, $/\wedge(\text{tall } x, \text{obnoxious } x)/ = 0.6$, and thus each of the three persons would contribute equally to the truth value of *Some tall persons are obnoxious* under the analysis that Lakoff assumes. However, that is counterintuitive: Sam is more relevant than Jack to the proposition that some tall persons are obnoxious, in that you would do a better job of proving that some tall persons are obnoxious by exhibiting Sam than by exhibiting Jack (with Fred being intermediate in his value as an exhibit).

One unusual feature of (11) is that it allows *Some f's are g's* to have a different truth value than *Some g's are f's*. Note that in the last example, Sam would make more of a contribution to the truth value of *Some tall persons are obnoxious* (namely 0.45) than he would to the truth value of *Some obnoxious persons are tall* (namely 0.12); thus, in a world peopled by Sams and Jacks but not by Freds, *Some tall persons are obnoxious* would be more true than *Some obnoxious persons are tall*. On reflection, I find this difference reasonable: Sam is of much more relevance to a statement about tall persons than to a statement about obnoxious persons. (11), like (9), includes the classical truth conditions as a special case: in the classical case, $/fx/(/fx/ + /gx/ - 1)$ has the value 1 when $/fx/ = /gx/ - 1$ and the value 0 otherwise, and thus the existential proposition has the truth value 1 when there is an individual such that $/fx/ = /gx/ = 1$ and has the value 0 otherwise.

The proposed truth conditions have the peculiarity that they would allow *Some fat persons are fat* to have a lower truth value than *Some persons are fat*: in a utopian world in which no one is fat to a greater degree than 0.8, /Some persons are fat/ = 0.8, but /Some fat persons are fat/ = 0.48. However, the existence of a truth value discrepancy between *Some persons are fat* and *Some fat persons are fat* is reasonable if one compares *Some fat persons are fat* with such sentences as *Some fat persons have good hearing* and *Some fat persons are intelligent*. Suppose that in this utopian world in which no one is fat to a degree greater than 0.8, no one is intelligent to a degree less than 0.9 or has good hearing to a degree less than 0.9. Then *Some fat persons are intelligent* and *Some fat persons have good hearing* ought to have greater truth value than *Some fat persons are fat*, since anyone in this world has good hearing and is intelligent to a greater degree than he is fat. By contrast, *All fat persons are fat* will have the truth value 1, regardless of who is how fat. But that fact is no cause for alarm, since in the utopian situation of this example, *All fat persons have good hearing* will also have the truth value 1.

However, some of the figures that I have given, such as the figure of 0.48 for the truth value of *Some fat persons are fat* when there are persons up to 0.8 fat, raise a real cause for worry, namely that the proposed truth conditions may be systematically assigning to existential propositions truth values that are too low. In fact, the expression $/fx/(/fx/ + /gx/ - 1)$ can be zero or negative far too easily for it to be an acceptable measure of 'the degree to which *x* is an *f* which *g*'. In particular, if $/fx/ + /gx/ = 1$, then the expression equals 0, which presumably ought to mean that a person who is tall to degree 0.4 and obnoxious to degree 0.6 is to degree 0 a tall person who is obnoxious. While he isn't a tall person who is obnoxious to a very large degree, he surely ought to be that to some degree. For the present, at least, I throw up my hands. While there are algebraic expressions galore that would give a greater truth value to 'the degree to which *x* is an *f* which *g*' in such cases, I do not have one to exhibit which provides a basis for revising the truth conditions for the universal quantifier in such a way that (a) the de Morgan laws remain valid, (b) the truth conditions include the classical truth conditions as a special case, and (c) the truth conditions for the universal quantifier embody a reasonable measure of 'counterexamplehood'.

The following are a system of rules of inference for quantifiers that fit the classical truth conditions, restated in terms of restricted quantification:

(13) ∀-expl
$(\forall x{:}fx)gx$
fa
ga

∃-expl
$(\exists x{:}fx)gx$
| fu
| gu
|———
| . . .
| A
A

∀-intro
| fu
|———
| . . .
| gu
$(\forall x{:}fx)gx$

∃-intro
fa
ga
$(\exists x;fx)gx$

Two of these rules, namely ∃-expl and ∀-intro, fit the truth conditions (9) and (11), in the sense that if they yield a conclusion that is less true that all of the operative premises, then the same will also be true of the subordinate proof, and thus the blame for the 'unsoundness' of the inference can be shifted onto some step of the subordinate proof. This is proved in Appendix B. However, the other two rules of inference obviously do not fit the truth conditions, as is shown by the following possible truth values for the relevant propositions:

(14)	$(\forall x{:}fx)gx$	0.92	(where *a* is the best
	fa	0.4	example of 'an *f* which
	ga	0.2	is not a *g*')
	fb	0.8	(where *b* is the best
	gb	0.8	example of 'an *f*
	$(\exists x{:}fx)gx$	0.48	which is a *g*')

It is dismaying that of the four rules for quantifiers, the two that clearly do not fit the truth conditions that I have proposed here are the two that a logician would be most willing to stake his life on. A dilemma now arises. If ∀-expl is to yield conclusions of truth value not less than that of all the premises, then a universal proposition can have at most the truth value that (1) and (8) would assign to it. If $/fa/ > /ga/$, then for the truth conditions to fit ∀-expl, $/(\forall x;fx)gx/$ can be at most $/ga/$, since otherwise both premises in the inference via ∀-expl would have truth value greater than the conclusion; since in that case $/\supset(fa, ga)/ = /ga/$, and since if $/fa/ \leq /ga/$, $/\supset(fa, ga)/ = 1$, then no matter what *a* is, the truth value of the universal $\leq /\supset(fa, ga)/$, which is to say

$$(15) \qquad /(\forall x{:}fx)gx/ \leq \min_x /\supset(fx, gx)/.$$

But then ∀-expl can only fit truth conditions that make a universal proposition less true than I've argued it ought to be in cases like the Nelson Rockefeller case. This means that if universal propositions are to have as high a truth value as I have argued for, I will have to either give up ∀-expl in favor of some weaker rule of inference or accept some less stringent criterion of fit between rules of inference and principles of truth value assignment. While I find giving up ∀-expl by far the less attractive of these two alternatives, I also feel quite uneasy about the other alternative, especially in view of the fact that it was not particularly difficult to find truth conditions for the propositional connectives which fit virtually all of the natural deduction rules of classical propositional logic, under this stringent criterion of fit.

Propositions $(\forall x{:}fx)gx$ in which *f* can take on non-classical truth values constitute one of the few cases where I can see some point in a 'normative' attitude which would either condemn some natural language usages as logically incoherent or maintain that in all supposed instances of those usages the speaker really means something else. The difficulty with applying ∀-exploitation or ∃-introduction is that both rules hinge upon the notion of 'special case' or 'particular instance', but when *f* is a fuzzy predicate it is not clear what should count as an 'instance' of *fx* for which *gx*. Here a striking difference between quantification and conjunction/disjunction appears. Quantifiers are often thought of as 'big conjunctions/disjunctions' (or conjunctions and disjunctions are thought of as little quantifiers). However, in any conjunction or disjunction, no matter how fuzzy the constituent propositions are, there is no fuzziness as to what constituent propositions it is made up of: any particular proposition either is one of the conjuncts or is not one of the conjuncts, and the possibility of its being 'sort of a conjunct' does not arise. By contrast, in the case of $(\forall x{:}fx)gx$ or of $(\exists x{:}fx)gx$, where *fx* is 'fuzzy', the proposition can be regarded as a 'big conjunction/disjunction' only by admitting fuzziness as to what the conjuncts are. Does *All fat persons are jolly* cover the case of Marlon Brando? of Nelson Rockefeller? Not only can an absolute answer of *Yes* or *No* not be given here, but an answer of *Sort of* or *Somewhat* would be quite bizarre, as well as not being true. Whether a given special case *a* for which $/fa/ < 1$ is taken in depends on what the speaker intended to be taken in. If he intends the universal proposition to be taken so broadly as to include Brando, fine. If he intends it to be taken even more broadly, so as to include Rockefeller, also fine. However, it is up to him to make clear what is to be taken in, and for any particular decision on his part, the truth value of the quantified proposition will presumably be determined by the value of $/gx/$ within the domain that he has taken the quantified proposition to cover. If the truth value of the quantified proposition is taken to be $\min_x /gx/$ for the universal, and $\max_x /gx/$ for the existential, we will have the truth conditions that would arise were we to replace *fx* by a function that is 1 or 0 in accordance with the broadness of the speaker's conception of 'special case', and then assign truth values in accordance with (1) and (6). This proposal is merely a terminological variant of the normative logician's suggestion that a person who says *All fat persons are jolly* really means something else, namely that all persons whose fatness exceeds some fixed degree are jolly. (It should be emphasized that fuzziness in *gx* creates no problems whatever; thus a normative logician can demand that *All fat persons are jolly* be supplied with something more precise than *fat person* as a specification of the domain of the quantifier, without his necessarily having any scruples about fuzzy predicates in general.) Under this approach, the difference between Marlon Brando and Nelson Rockefeller is not that they reduce the truth value of *All fat persons are jolly* by different amounts. In any case in which they both affect its truth value (i.e. in any case in which the speaker interprets *all fat persons* so broadly as to take in not only Brando but also Rockefeller), they place the same upper limit on its truth value. The difference is that it takes a much less broad interpretation of *all fat persons* for Brando to have this effect than for Rockefeller to have it.[8]

This approach differs from those considered earlier, with respect to a case that has hitherto seemed quite uninteresting. Suppose that /Kissinger is fat/ = 0.5 and /Kissinger is jolly/ = 0.6. Then for x = Kissinger, $/\supset(fx, gx)/ = 1$ and $/fx/(/fx/ - /gx/) = -0.05$. Thus, under both proposals considered earlier, Kissinger would not reduce /All fat persons are jolly/ (i.e. it could still be 1 despite the existence of persons like Kissinger). On the other hand, under the proposal of the last paragraph, if the domain of the bound variable were interpreted broadly enough to include Kissinger, /All fat persons are jolly/ could be at most 0.6, since Kissinger would be a member of the domain for which /jolly x/ was 0.6. In addition, the truth value of *All fat persons are fat* would no longer necessarily be 1: the broader the domain that the bound variable is taken to range over, the lower the truth value of *All fat persons are fat* will be. By now I have considered so many possibilities for the truth values of these sentences that my opinions as to the reasonableness of any particular values should not be taken too seriously; at least I would say that the truth values yielded by the proposal of the last paragraph are not obviously wrong.

APPENDIX A

Proof that $\supset$-intro fits the truth conditions (1). Suppose we have an inference with a conclusion $\supset AB$ that is derived by $\supset$-intro. Let $a = /A/$, $b = /B/$, and d = the minimum of the truth values of the premises of the (main) proof. If $a \leq b$, then the conclusion has truth value 1, and since $1 \geq d$, the conclusion has truth value at least that of the weakest premise. Suppose that $a > b$. Then $/\supset AB/ = b$. If the conclusion has lower truth value than the weakest premise, then $b < d$. The subordinate proof has as its operative premises A and the premises of the main proof; thus the truth value of the weakest premise operative in the subordinate proof is $\min(a, d)$. Since b is less than both a and d and is the truth value of the conclusion of the subordinate proof, the subordinate proof has a conclusion of lower truth value than all of the premises that are operative in it. Thus, a conclusion derived by ⊃-intro can be of lower truth value than the weakest operative premise only if the subordinate proof also has a conclusion that is of lower truth value than the weakest premise that is operative in the subproof. Thus, if a proof whose conclusion is inferred by ⊃-intro is unsound, the blame for the unsoundness can be shifted off of ⊃-intro and onto one of the steps in the subordinate proof.

Proof that ∨-expl fits the truth conditions (1): Suppose that we have a proof whose conclusion is inferred by ∨-expl, with truth values as indicated:

```
Premises    d = /weakest premise/
. . .
∨AB         max(a, b)
   | A      a
   |-----
   | . . .
   | C      c
   | B      b
   |-----
   | . . .
   | C      c
  C         c
```

(Actually, ∨*AB* might be among the premises; however, we could then apply reiteration so as to get an occurrence of ∨*AB* which was not among the 'premises', so there is no loss of generality in this diagram.) Suppose that in both of the subproofs, the conclusion is of truth value at least that of the weakest operative premise, i.e. $c \geq \min(a, d)$ and $c \geq \min(b, d)$. In that case $c \geq \min(\max(a, b), d)$. Then the only way that the main proof could have a conclusion lower in truth value than the premise (i.e. $c < d$) would be for $\max(a, b) \leq c < d$. But since $\max(a, b) = /\vee AB/$, the step in which $<AB$ is inferred would have a truth value lower than all the operative premises. Hence, any unsoundness in an inference whose conclusion is drawn by ∨-expl can be blamed on an earlier step of the proof.

APPENDIX B

Proof that ∀-intro fits the truth conditions (1) and (9). Suppose we have a proof whose conclusion is drawn by ∀-intro and whose conclusion is of lower truth value than the weakest premise:

Premises d = /weakest premise/

. . .

| *fu*
|———
| *gu*

$(\forall x{:}fx)gx$

Let a be a value of x which maximizes $/fx/(/fx/ - /g/)$. Let $b = /fa/$ and $c = /ga/$. Then the truth value of the conclusion is $1 - b(b - c)$, and that is less than d. Suppose that the steps other than the last step of the proof are 'sound', in the sense that no instance of that step leads to a conclusion of lower truth value than the weakest premise that is operative in the step in question. Then the following proof is 'sound':

fa	b
Premises as above	d = /weakest premise/
. . .	
. . .	
ga	c

and thus $c \geq \min(b, d)$. *Case 1*. Suppose that $c \geq b$. Then $b - c \leq 0$, and so $1 - b(b - c) \geq 1$. But $d > 1 - b(b - c)$, and thus $d > 1$, which is impossible, since d is a truth value. *Case 2*. Suppose that $c < b$. Then $c \geq d$ (since $c \geq \min(b, d)$). Since $d > 1 - b(b - c)$, we then have

$$c > 1 - b^2 + bc$$
$$c - bc > 1 - b^2$$
$$c(1 - b) > (1 + b)(1 - b)\ .$$

Let us separate two subcases. *Case 2a*. Suppose $b < 1$. Then we can cancel $1 - b$ from both sides of the inequality and obtain $1 + b < c$. But $b \geq 0$, which implies that $c > 1$, which is impossible. *Case 2b*. Suppose $b = 1$. Then $d > 1 - b(b - c)$ becomes $d > 1 - 1 + c$, i.e. $d > c$. But this contradicts our conclusion that $c \geq d$. Thus, the assumption that unsoundness comes in only in the final step of the proof leads to a contradiction.

Proof that ∃-expl fits the truth conditions (1) and (11). Suppose that we have a proof whose conclusion is inferred by ∃-expl and whose conclusion is of lower truth value than any of the operative premises:

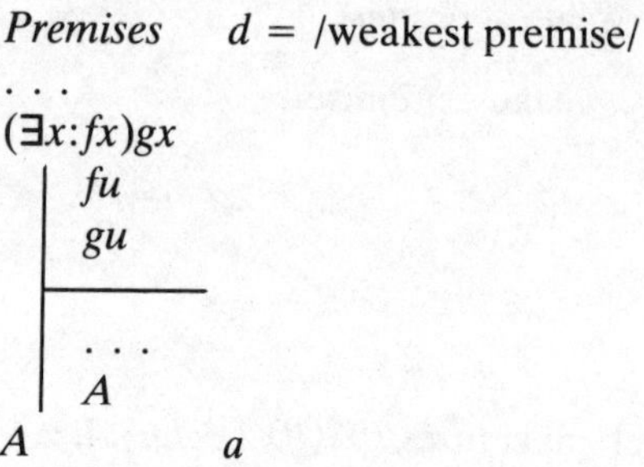

(As before, there is no loss of generality from taking the existential to be separate from the 'Premises'.) Let e be an element which maximizes $/fx/(/fx/ + /gx/ - 1)$, and let $b = /fe/$, $c = /ge/$. Then the truth value of the existential is $b(b + c - 1)$, and if the application of ∃-exploitation is what is responsible for the unsoundness of the whole argument, we have $a < d \leq b(b + c - 1)$. If the unsoundness of the whole proof is due to the final step, the the following proof is sound:

Premises as before d = /weakest premise/
fe b
ge c
. . .
. . .
A a

Since b and c are both at most 1, $b(b + c - 1)$ is less than or equal to both b and c. Since we have $d \leq b(b + c - 1)$, we thus have $d \leq b$ and $d \leq c$, and hence the weakest premise of the last proof has truth value d. But since $a > d$, that means that the last argument has a conclusion of lower truth value than its weakest premise and is thus unsound. But since the steps in the latter argument are merely the steps prior to the final step in the original argument, we have shown that any unsoundness in the original argument must be due to some step other than its last step.

NOTES

* The paper entitled 'Presupposition and Discourse Structure' that I read at the Uppsala University 500th Anniversary Symposium on Philosophy and Grammar will appear in D. Dineen and Choon-Kyu Oh (eds.), *Presupposition* (= *Syntax and Semantics* 11), to be published by Academic Press, New York. In its place I have substituted the present paper, which I presented on Oct. 11, 1975, at the Vancouver Symposium on Semantics, organized by the philosophy departments of Simon Fraser University and the University of Victoria. I am grateful to the participants, especially to Bas van Fraassen and F. J. Pelletier, for their stimulating comments.

[1] See Lakoff (1972) for considerations suggesting that the truth values for at least some kinds of propositions should be complexes of 'simple' truth values, with each coordinate representing a different kind or aspect of truth (e.g. 'literal applicability' as one coordinate and 'connotative applicability' as another). See also Herzberger (1973, 1975) on multidimensional truth values.

[2] I will restrict myself to the case where only '1' is a 'designated' truth value.

[3] I do not mean to suggest by this that I have any strong affection for truth-functionality. See McCawley (1975) for a specification of the extent to which deviations from truth-functionality in 2-valued logic are consistent with the rules of natural deducation presented here. I hope eventually to solve the same problem for multi-valued logics.

Throughout this paper, through force of habit, I follow the 'Polish' practise of writing connectives before rather than between the items that they connect, though I use Anglo-American and not Polish symbols for the connectives (i.e. I write $\supset pq$ rather than either $p \supset q$ or Cpq). My adoption of a type of 'Polish' notation is due to my conviction (McCawley, 1972) that $\wedge$ and $\vee$ are not 2-place connectives but rather connect any number of propositions at a time. Since I take logical structures to have the formal nature of trees rather than strings of symbols, I regard parentheses as merely an informal convenience to aid the reader in apprehending the intended constituent structure. I thus do not avail myself of the possibility of 'parenthesis-free' formulas that 'Polish notation' affords; of course, if $\wedge$ and $\vee$ combine with arbitrarily many sentences rather than a fixed number at a time, the notation is no longer fully 'parenthesis-free', i.e. formulas can differ in constituent structure without differing in the sequence of variables and connectives that they contain, e.g. $\wedge(\vee pq, r, s) \neq \wedge(\vee pqr, s)$.

[4] I have adopted the term 'exploitation' in preference to Fitch's term 'elimination', since the connective in question is not really 'eliminated': the earlier line that is made use of in an application of $\wedge$-exploitation, $\supset$-exploitation, etc. remains part of the proof and can perfectly well serve as justification for later steps in the proof.

[5] Actually, the formulas should be in terms of 'greatest lower bound' and 'least upper bound' rather than 'minimum' and 'maximum'; however, to simplify the discussion, I will act as if 'minimum' and 'maximum' were what was involved. Thus, strictly speaking, the proofs in appendix B should be replaced by more complicated proofs in which it is not assumed that any element maximizes or minimizes the expression under discussion.

[6] Lakoff in fact adopted different truth conditions for $\supset$: when $/A/ > /B/$, he took $/\supset AB/$ to be 0 rather than $/B/$. The problem that I am about to discuss arises even more blatantly when those truth conditions are assumed.

[7] For convenience sake, I will take the universe of discourse to contain only persons and will thus ignore the contribution of *person* to the meanings and truth conditions of the examples.
[8] If this proposal stands up, then the truth-values can be less real-number like than I have assumed, since one no longer need be able to perform algebraic operations on truth values (e.g. to compute $/fx/(/fx/ - /gx/)$, other than that of computing $1 - /A/$.

BIBLIOGRAPHY

Anderson, A. R. and N. Belnap: 1975, *Entailment*, Vol. 1 (Princeton University Press, Princeton).

Haack, Susan: 1975, *Deviant Logics* (Cambridge University Press, London).

Herzberger, Hans: 1973, 'Dimensions of Truth', *Journal of Philosophical Logic* **2, 535–556** Also in Hockney *et al.* (1975), 71–92.

Herzberger, Hans: 1975, 'Supervaluations in Two Dimensions', *Proceedings of the 1975 International Symposium on Multiple-Valued Logic* (IEEE, Long Beach), 429–435.

Hockney, D., W. Harper, and B. Freed: 1975, *Contemporary Research in Philosophical Logic and Linguistic Semantics* (Reidel, Dordrecht).

Kripke, Saul: 1959, 'A Completeness Theorem in Modal Logic', *Journal of Symbolic Logic* **24,** 1–15.

Kripke, Saul: 1963, 'Semantical Considerations on Modal Logic', *Acta Philosophica Fennica* **16,** 83–94.

Lakoff, George: 1972, 'Hedges: A Study in Meaning Criteria and the Logic of Fuzzy Concepts', *Paper from the 8th Regional Meeting, Chicago Linguistic Society*, 183–228. Corrected version appears in the *Journal of Philosophical Logic* (1973), **2,** 458–508 and in Hockney *et al.* (1975), 221–271.

Lewis, David: 1974, *Counterfactuals* (Harvard University Press, Cambridge, Mass.).

McCawley, James D.: 1972, 'A Program for Logic', in D. Davidson and G. Harman (eds.), *Semantics of Natural Language* (Reidel, Dordrecht), 498–544.

McCawley, James D.: 1975, 'Truth Functionality and Natural Deduction', *Proceedings of the 1975 International Symposium on Multiple-Valued Logic* (IEEE, Long Beach), 412–418.

Rescher, Nicholas: 1969, *Many-Valued Logics* (McGraw Hill, New York).

W. ADMONI

DIE SEMANTISCHE STRUKTUR DER SYNTAKTISCHEN GEBILDE UND DIE SEMANTISCHEN SYSTEME DER GENERATIVISTEN

ABSTRACT The principle of separating form and meaning in grammar on the grounds that there is no one-to-one correspondence between them is unjustified and leads to the wrong position that form is inherently devoid of content. There is to each morphological or syntactical form (e.g. a case form or a sentence type) a centre of meaning around which are grouped other variants of content in a field-like way. In the speech-chain there is a multidimensional grammatical semantics which is organized as a complicated pattern of interaction between the semantics of world-class, morphology, syntax, context, and situation, respectively. The language-specific structuring of this interaction is the object of grammatical research. For this research sets of features as postulated by semantics-oriented directions within generative grammar can be a most valuable tool as long as they are considered as such and not as semantic systems with an existence of their own. Since they have been established by way of systematizing results from inductive analysis of real languages, induction takes primacy over deduction, and any attempt to unadjustedly regard such sets of features as the semantic basis for existant grammatical forms in a specific language is a violation of the structure of that language. This criticism holds true for all semantic systems put forward within generative grammar because of its separation of syntax and semantics. Thereby the attested grammatical forms are degraded to purely formal, asemantic, surface structure shapes, although they, as described above, in reality form a multidimensional system of grammatical meaning in the speech-chain. The claim of absolutism for generative grammar is detrimental to grammatical science. For systematizing inductively established knowledge, however, the use of sets of features as well as of transformations can be of great help but it should be regarded as one of several methods within grammatical theory.

Es herrscht in den letzten Jahrzehnten in der Linguistik die Tendenz, die Semantik der grammatischen Formen von diesen Formen abzusondern und die beiden Erscheinungen (d.h. die Semantik und die grammatischen Formen) getrennt zu behandeln. Hervorgerufen wurde diese Tendenz einerseits durch die allgemeine semiotische Einstellung, die Syntax (d.h. das Formengebiet) von der Semantik (und der Pragmatik) zu trennen. Anderseits war hier die Tatsache wirksam, daß die Beziehungen der grammatischen Form zu der von ihr ausgedrückten Semantik sehr kompliziert sind. Die Form und die Semantik decken einander in der Regel nicht; sie sind, wie es S. Karcevsky formuliert hat, asymmetrisch.[1]

Aber bei genauer Prüfung sind diese beiden Begründungen der prinzipiellen Trennung der formalen von der semantischen Komponente in der Grammatik nicht stichhaltig.

S. Kanger and S. Öhman (eds.), Philosophy and Grammar, 119–133

Was die allgemeinen semiotischen Erwägungen betrifft, so scheitern sie an der Tatsache, daß die natürliche menschliche Sprache keinen Code im eigentlichen Sinne des Wortes darstellt, sondern ein viel komplizierteres System, das mit dem menschlichen Leben auf außerordentlich vielfältige Art verbunden ist – sowohl mit der gesellschaftlichen Existenz des Menschen als auch mit seinem Innenleben. Die natürliche Sprache hat so viele Funktionen unter solch verschiedenen Umständen zu erfüllen, daß man von vornherein annehmen darf, daß sie mit der gewöhnlichen einfachen Code-Struktur auszukommen nicht imstande ist. Was aber die Asymmetrie der grammatischen Semantik betrifft, so bedeutet solche Asymmetrie keineswegs, daß den grammatischen Formen die Semantik überhaupt fehlt. Die Asymmetrie ist ja durchaus nicht mit einem Mangel an jeglicher Strukturierung identisch. Auch symmetrische Strukturen sind in verschiedenen Bereichen des Seins möglich, Nur, daß es komplizierte, zuweilen sogar schwer zu erfassende Strukturen sind. Aber eben das schwer zu Erfassende bildet ja heute den eigentlichen Untersuchungsgegenstand der modernen Wissenschaft.

Deswegen wirkt es befremdend, wenn heute, wie übrigens bereits häufig schon vor vielen Jahren,[2] die Existenz des verallgemeinerten Bedeutungsgehalts der grammatischen Formen im Deutschen aus dem Anlaß geleugnet wird, daß z.B. der Akkusativ in manchen Fällen auch bei solchen Verben zu stehen hat, die nicht die Semantik einer aktiven, das Objekt unmittelbar berührenden, umfassenden oder erzeugenden Handlung aufweisen. Daß es semantisch andersgeartete Verbindungen des Verbs mit dem Akkusativ wirklich gibt, steht außer Zweifel. Aber der Hinweis auf solche Fälle sollte ja den Forscher nur veranlassen, alle Bedingungen sorgfältig zu prüfen, die bei der Bildung solcher Fügungen im Spiele sind, die Möglichkeit der Einwirkung von verschiedenen Faktoren dabei in Erwägung zu ziehen usw. Aber in der Regel wird das alles nicht getan. Die Feststellung der Diskrepanz zwischen der Form und der Semantik genügt, um die grammatische Form überhaupt als ganz gehaltlos zu kennzeichnen, als eine leere Hülle, die sich je nach dem Bedürfnis durch verschiedenartige diskrete Bedeutungsgehalte füllen läßt. So wird der Weg bereitet für die Dependenzgramatiken, die in ihrer radikalen Form den Satz nur als ein Gebilde von formalen Abhängigkeitsstrukturen betrachten, ohne auf die Semantik solcher Gebilde einzugehen, und für verschiedene generativistische Richtungen, die die konkreten, in der Rede tatsächlich gebrauchten syntaktischen Formen zu Oberflächenstrukturen degradieren, die nur durch Reduzierung zu

Tiefenstrukturen in ihrem Sinn zu erschließen sind.

In Wirklichkeit aber sind nicht nur die grammatischen Formen mit einer bestimmten Semantik ausgerüstet, sondern diese Semantik bildet (in jeder Sprache auf ihre eigene Art) ein gewisses System, stellt eine komplizierte Struktur dar.

Hier, in meinem Aufsatz, läßt sich diese Struktur selbstverständlich nur ganz schematisch und thesenartig charakterisieren. Ubrigens habe ich über manche dazugehörenden Erscheinungen bereits mehrmals geschrieben.[3] Allerdings muß ich hier einen Vorbehalt machen: es können gewiß in verschiedenen Sprachen auch einzelne grammatische Formen vorkommen, die des semantischen Gehalts entbehren. Aber es sind nur Randerscheinungen, Ausnahmen. Normalerweise ist einer grammatischen Form ein Bedeutungsgehalt eigen.[4]

Ich beginne mit der eindimensionalen (eigentlich: interaspektischen) Struktur des Bedeutungsgehalts von grammatischen Formen. Es wird hier somit nur solche Semantik betrachtet, die nur zu einer semantischen (oder semantisch-funktionalen) Dimension (zu einem Aspekt) gehört.

Die eindimensionale Semantik ist sowohl bei den morphologischen als auch bei den syntaktischen Formen vorhanden (z.B. in der Morphologie bei den Redeteilen oder bei den Kasusformen, in der Syntax z.B. bei den durch syntaktische Dependenz gebildeten Satzmodellen, die ich logisch-grammatische Satztypen nenne.)

Allerdings wird auf dem Gebiet der Kasusbedeutungen die Ausrüstung der grammatischen Formen durch Semantik aufs heftigste bestritten. Aber selbst hier, wo manes in der Regel in solchen Sprachen wie der deutschen oder der russischen wirklich mit verblüffender Buntheit und manchen Widersprüchen zu tun hat, wird das Bild durchsichtiger und geregelter, wenn man verschiedene Gebrauchs- und Fügungsarten der Kasusformen auseinanderhält, z.B. den Gebrauch der obliquen Kasus mit und ohne Präpositionen, den Gebrauch des Genitivs als Attribut und als Objekt usw. Und die Wiedersprüche, die selbst innerhalb ein und desselben syntaktischen Gebrauchs gewisser Kasusformen doch zu verzeichnen sind, lassen sich zum größten Teil erklären durch die Einwirkung von verschiedenen konkreten Faktoren, im Bereiche der verbalen Rektion besonders durch die Präfigierung, da einige verbale Präfixe einen bestimmten Objektkasus fast automatisch fordern. Auch die Anwesenheit im Elementarsatz gewisse anderer Komponenten kann zuweilen zu semantischen Verlagerungen in dem Bedeutungsgehalt der Objektskasusformen führen.

Da befinden wir uns aber bereits auf dem Gebiete der syntaktischen Strukturen, nämlich der logisch-grammatischen Satztypen, und da kann ich mich, um Zeit zu sparen, auf zwei Aufsätze berufen, wo diese Fragen in Bezug auf die deutschen Satztypen mit dem Akkusativ- und Dativobjekt eingehend erörtet werden.[5] Doch ist es notwendig, auch hier auf das allgemeine Prinzip hinzuweisen, das der Struktur der Semantik der betreffenden logisch-grammatischen Satztypen zugrunde liegt. Es herrscht hier nämlich die Feldstruktur, was übrigens überhaupt für die grammatischen Erscheinungen kennzeichnend ist.[6]

Es gibt ja einen derartigen Bereich innerhalb der Masse von Realisierungen jedes Satztyps, in dem der verallgemeinerte Bedeutungsgehalt des betreffenden Satztyps klar auftritt und dem anderer logisch-grammatischer Satztypen gegenübergestellt wird. Auf dem Gebiete der Satztypen mit der Objektsemantik findet dies bei den Verben mit der Semantik des Gebens und Erzählens statt, die je mit zwei Objekten, im Dativ und im Akkusativ, verbunden werden.

Dieser Bereich bildet nun das Zentrum (genauer: die Zentren) beider Felder, und alle übrigen Realisierungen dieser Satztypen gruppieren sich um sie, zum Teil semantisch mit ihnen zusammenfallend oder ziemlich nahestehend, zum Teil sich bedeutend daren entfernend. So bildet sich bei beiden Typen eine weite Peripherie, an welcher sich in einigen Fällen, besonders wenn gewisse Formstützen vorhanden sind, gewisse Untertypen oder sogar neue logisch-grammatische Satztypen entwickeln. Als solche sind wohl die Konstruktionen *Es gibt* + Akkusativ und *haben* + Akkusativ zu betrachten. Die erste von diesen Konstruktionen drückt ja die Existenz des durch den Akkusativ bezeichneten Gegenstands aus, die zweite in mehreren Fällen (bei entsprechender semantischer Füllung des Akkusativs) den Zustünd des durch den Nominativ bezeichneten Subjekts.

Wenn man somit die eindimensionale Semantik der grammatischen Formen als Feldstruktur betrachtet, so stellt sie sich als eine kompliziert strukturierte Erscheinung dar, aber bei sorgfältiger Betrachtung läßt sie sich in der Regel wenigstens in ihren Hauptumrissen bestimmen. Und in vielen Fällen ist die Feldstruktur der eindimensionalen Semantik von grammatischen Formen überhaupt nicht so verworren wie in dem eben geschilderten Falle. So sind z.B. in semantischer Hinsicht viel leichter durchschauber die logisch-grammatischen Satztypen, die mit dem Substantivprädikativ im Nominativ und mit Adjektivprädikat gebildet werden.[7]

Es gibt selbstverständlich auch andere semantische Dimensionen außer der, die wir eben betrachtet haben, und die letzten Endes in der Referenzbezogenheit (Sachbezogenheit) der grammatischen Formen auf die außerhalb des kommunikativen Redeskts liegende Welt besteht und die ich als die logisch-grammatische bezeichne. Es existieren außerdem auch solche grammatische Forman, deren Semantik verschiedene Beziehungen des Redenden zum Redeakt wiederspiegelt. Solche Semantik, die ich als kommunikativ-grammatisch bezeichnen würde,[8] besteht selbst aus vielen Dimensionen. So gibt es z.B. die modale semantische Diemsnionu, die die Einschätzung der Realität des in der Rede ausgedrückten Sachverhalts vom Standpunkt des Sprechenden ausdrückt und durch verschiedene grammatische Formen zum Ausdruck gebracht wird. Auch hier hat man in der Regel mit Feldstrukturen zu tun, sowohl was die Gestaltung des Bedeutungsgehalts der Formen betrifft, die als Träger der Modalitätsemantik auftreten, also auch darin, daß die verschiedenen, die Modalität zum Ausdruck bringenden grammatischen Formen und lexikalen Mittel zusammen ein besonderes Feld bilden, in dem die einzelnen Erscheinungen zusammenwirken können.[9] Es können auch Randerscheinungen vorkommen, wo z.B. innerhalb der Semantik einer grammatischen Form die logisch-grammatischen Bedeutungen sich mit den modalen berühren, was zu verschiedenen Komplikationen führen kann. So sind in einigen verbalen Formen die modale Semantik und die der Handlungsformen schwer von einander zu unterscheiden. Aber dies erschüttert die Existenz der monodimensionalen Semantik der grammatischen Formen keineswegs. Sondern es führt uns nur zu der anderen Region hinüber, in der die grammatische Semantik existiert, namentlich zu der multidimensionalen.[10] Und nur wenn wir such diese Region in unsere Betrachtungen miteinbeziehen, können wir die Gesamtstruktur der Semantik der grammatischen Formen überschauen.

Die multidimensionale Region der Semantik von grammatischen Formen teilt sich in zwei Unterregionen.

Einerseits gibt es multidimensionale (d.h. verschieden-aspektige) verallgemeinerte Bedeutungen, die an eine grammatische Form beständig geknüpft sind. So haven wir in der Morphologie in der Wortform *Wolfs* immer gleichzeitig mit folgenden grammatischen Bedeutungen zu tun: Maskulinium, Singular, Genitiv.

Ich will mich auf die Charakteristik dieser Bedeutungen hier nicht häher einlassen, sondern mich mit der Feststellung ihres Vorhandenseins begnügen und die Bedeutungen solcher Art weiter unten als beständige bezeichnen. Es ist nur hinzuzufügen, daß sie in komplizierten Beziehungen zueinander stehen. Ihre Grundlage wird von der verallgemeinerten Bedeutung der Wortarten gebildet, die von anderen verallgemeinerten Bedeutungen auf verschiedene Weise überlagert wird.

Andererseits gibt es solche verallgemeinerte grammatische Bedeutungen, die nur unter gewissen Bedingungen in der Redekette die betreffende grammatische Form zu überlagern imstande sind. Solche Bedeutungen dürfte mans als variable bezeichnen. Aber hier muß der Sachverhalt präzisiert werden.

Wenn man die morphologischen Formen als Ausgangspunkt nimmt, so ist z.B. die grammatische Bedeutung des Subjekts, die sich an die Form des Nominative in den betreffenden logisch-grammatischen Satztypen knüpft, eine variable, da im anderen syntaktischen Gebrauch der Nominativ eben von anderen syntaktischen Bedeutungen überlagert werden kann. Aber vom Standpunkt der syntaktischen Einheiten aus ist die dem Nominativ zukommende Bedeutung des Subjeckte eine beständige, die allerdings je nach dem logisch-grammatischen Satztypus semantisch verschiedenartig ausgerichtet ist. Da hier eben syntaktische Modelle, dem sprachlichen System angehörende syntaktische Strukturen auftreten, so sind auch die grammatischen Bedeutungen, die diesen Modellen innewohnen als beständige aufzufassen, somit sind, wie gesagt, auch die den Gliedern solcher Modelle innewohnenden Bedeutungen im syntaktischen Sinn beständig. Ich will sie dementsprechend also syntaktisch-bedingte Beständige grammatische Bedeutungen bezeichnen.

Dagegen gibt es im Satz, wie er im Text, in der dialogischen oder monologischen Rede auftritt, eine Reihe von grammatischen Bedeutungen, die in der Abhängigkeit von Kontext, von der Redesituation, von den Einstellungen und von dem emotionalen Zustand des Sprechenden verschiedenen Satzkomponenten zugeordnet werden können. Dies gilt z.B. für die sehr wichtigen Bedeutungen, die dem Aspekt der Erkenntniseinstellung (oder der kommunikativ-aktuellen gliederung des Satzes) angehören. Solche Bedeutungen wie das Bekannte (das Thema) und das Neue (das Rhema) können sich in einem mehrgliedrigen Satz auf verschiedene Weise verschieben.

Oft überlagert z.B. die Bedeutung des Neuen das Subjekt, aber sie kann auch das Objekt oder eine Adberbialbestimmung überlagern oder eine Verbindung von einigen Satzkomponenten usw. Auch solche

Bedeutungen, die dem Aspekt "die kommunikative Zieleinstellung des Sprechenden"[12] angehören, können sich auf verschiedene variierende Bestandteile des Satzes stützen.

So wird z.B. die Bedeutung des Fragesatzes (nämlich des Entscheidungssatzes) bereits mit dem Verb in der Anfangsstellung und den unmittelbar darauf folgenden Satzkomponenten in den Satz eingeführt und auf diese Weise den betreffenden Wortformen zugeordnet, obgleich an und für sich diese Wortformen solche Bedeutung nicht ausdrücken. Die Bedeutungen des Neuen, des Fragesatzes usw. sind somit variable grammatische Bedeutungen die je nach der Beschaffenheit des Satzes in seiner konkreten kommunikativen Funktion und Form seine verschiedenen Komponenten überlagern können.

Ich habe hier keine Möglichkeit, das Gebiet der variablen grammatischen Bedeutungen näher zu umreißen, noch auf verschiedene Komplikationen im Begriff der grammatischen Bedeutung einzugehen, die hier zum Vorschein kommen und die darin bestehen, daß die syntaktischen Funktionen selbst hier als besondere Abarten der grammatischen Bedeutung suftreten oder wenigstens zum Teil also solche betrachtet werden können. (Ich meine z.B. solche syntaktisch-funktionalen Bedeutungen wie die des Haupt- und Nebensatzes). Ich muß mich hier nur auf die Darstellung des Systems der variablen grammatischen Bedeutungen berufen, das ich mit geringen Änderungen vor Jahren entworfen habe. Anhand eines kurzen deutschen Satzes (*Ich hab'es heute dem Vater gesagt*) wurde dabei ein ganzes partiturartiges Gebilde der grammatischen Bedeutungen zusammengestellt und schematisch vorgeführt, in dem 14 Linien von grammatischen Bedeutungen den Wortformenbestand des Satzes überlagern. In dem Schema wurde auch dargestellt, wie die Wortstellung und die Intonation bei der Zuordnung der variablen grammatischen Bedeutungen zu den Wortformen wirksam sind und wie sich dabei auch die Berbindungen mit dem Kontext kundtun.[13]

Solche partiturartige Gestaltung ist eben die konkrete Form, in der das multidimensionale System der grammatischen Bedeutungen in der Rede auftritt. Sie bildet eigentlich eine besondere Region, in der die grammatischen Erscheinungen existieren, namentlich eine 'vertikale' oder 'mehrschichtige' Region, die ich als die 'batysmatische' bezeichnet habe (von gr. *batys* 'tief'), und die neben der paradigmatischen und der syntagmatischen Region der grammatischen Erscheinungen auftritt. Man dürfte wohl diese drei Regionen als Hauptdimensionen des grammatischen Systems bezeichnen, d.h. als seine Dimensionen höheren Crades. Das batysmatische System hat die verallgemeinerten Bedeutungen der Wortarten zu seiner Grundlage. Darauf ruhen die anderen morphologischen beständigen grammatischen Bedeutungen, die ihrerseits von den syntaktischen beständigen und letzten Endes von den variablen grammatischen Bedeutungen überlagert werden. Dabei sind die eindimensionalen grammatischen Bedeutungen in der Regel auf komplizierte Weise strukturiert, weisen nämlich Feldstruktur auf.

Die eigentliche Erfassung der grammatischen Semantik irgendeiner Sprache besteht somit darin, daß man dieses System der Semantik der grammatischen Formen in seiner ganzen komplizierten Konkretheit, d.h. in allen seinen Zusammenhängen erforscht. Nun aber bedient man sich bei der Erforschung von grammatischen Bedeutungen gewisser Vorstellungen und Begriffe, die auf verschiedene Weise zum Ausdruck gebracht werden. Ihrem Wesen nach sind diese Vorstellungen und Begriffe verschiedener Natur. Zum Teil sind diese Begriffe syntaktischer oder psychologischer oder logischer Natur (im Sinne von alter formaler Aristotelischer Logit). So z.B. die Bedeutungen des 'Bekannten' (des Themas) und des 'Neuen' (des Rhemas). Aber zum Teil sind sie ontologischer Natur, d.h. sind letzten Endes, durch die Vermittlung der Vorstellungen und der Begriffe des menschlichen Denkens, auf die Dinge und Geschehnisse der objektiven Welt ausgerichtet.

Dies ist nicht nur bei allen logisch-grammatischen Bedeutungen der Fall, sondern auch bei den meisten kommunikativ-grammatischen, da die Redesituation als solche auch durchaus ontologisch, als eine objektiv in verschiedenen Gestaltungen wiederkehrende Erscheinung aufzufassen ist. Es ist dabei sehr wichtig, daß dieselben ontologischen Erscheinungen als grammatische Bedeutungen oder als Bestandteile von grammatischen Bedeutungen mehrerer grammatischer Formen vorkommen. Noch wichtiger ist es, daß viele dieser grammatischen Bedeutungen in analogen oder nicht anologen grammatischen Formen in den verschiedensten Sprachen ausgedrückt werden.

Deswegen ist es selbstverständlich, daß seit der Antike alle grammatischen Theorien mehr oder weniger bestimmte Termini gebrauchten, um irgendwelche grammatischen Bedeutungen irgendwelcher grammatischen Formen zu bezeichnen. Sehr oft ist es in sehr beschränktem Ausmaß (fast ausschließlich im Bereich der Morphologie), unsystematisch und in sehr naiver Weise geschehen. Zum Teil wurden dabei die Begriffe der Aristotelischen, im 19.Jh., auch der

Hegelsschen Logik verwertet. Auch die Psychologie wurde in der neueren Zeit zur Formulierung der grammatischen Bedeutungen von grammatischen Formen herangezogen. Aber erst im 20.Jh. beginnt im weitesten Ausmaß die systematische Erforschung der grammatischen Bedeutungen. Besonders stark wirkt sich diese Tendenz in verschiedenen semantisch ausgerichteten Strömungen der Generativistik aus. Hier bildet diese Problematik den Mittelpunkt und den eigentlichen Gehalt der betreffenden Theorien, was sich auch als Reaktion auf den eine Zeitlang in dem amerikanischen. Strukturalismus vorherrschenden Antimentalismus verstehan läßt. Und die Tendenz zur gründlichen und systematischen Erfassung des komplizierten Bereichs von grammatischen Bedeutungen ist gewiß sehr lobenswert. Aber zwei Dinge sollte man dabei doch micht vergessen.

Alle als besondere Einheiten aufgestellten Systeme der grammatischen Bedeutungen, soweit sie eben als sprachwissenschaftliche, zur Grammatik gehörende Systeme auftreten wollen, sind ja doch nicht Selbstzweck, sondern Hilfskonstruktionen, dienen als Hilfsmittel für die bessere Erforschung des Systems der Bedeutungen von grammatischen Formen als solchen. Und zweitens dürfen diese Systeme nie ihre Verbundenheit mit den reell in den grammatischen Formen einer Sprache oder einiger Sprachen tatsächlich existierenden grammatischen Bedeutungen verleugnen. Sie müssen sich immer ihrer Herkunft aus den konkreten grammatischen Strukturen bewußt bleiben. Letzten Endes sind sie ja nichts anderes als systematisierte Listen, als logisch organisierte Thesauren von solcher Bedeutungen. Somit sind sie induktiv und sollten letzten Endes für jede Sprache eine – und sollte es auch nur in Einzelheiten sein – besondere Gestalt annehmen. Und was die Begriffe betrifft, die bei der Aufstellung von solchen induktiven Thesauren zu gebrauchen sind, so sollen sie grundsätzlich den Erscheinungen und Beziehungen der objektiven Welt entnommen sein, was auch zum Teil in der Form geschehen kann, die solche Erscheinungen und Bedeutungen in gewissen. Speziallogiken, z.B. in der Relationslogik gefunden haben. Man darf aber dabei nicht vergessen, daß es letzten Endes eben die Erscheinungen und Beziehungen der objektiven Welt sind, die – oft in gebrochener Form unter verschiedenen Gesichtswinkeln – in dem Gehalt der grammatischen Formen ihren Niederschlag finden.

Deswegen ist es kein Zufall, daß die grammatischen Bedeutungen in den verschiedensten Sprachen außerordentlich viel gemeinsam haben. Wie ich bereits vor vierzig Jahren geschrieben habe, "kommen im

Satz. . . einige für den gesellschaftlichen Menschen besonders wichtige Gesetzmäßigkeiten der objektiven Wirklichkeit zum Ausdruck, wobei sie nicht nur durch den Gehalt des Satzes, sondern auch durch seine Form ausgedrückt werden."[14] Es ist ja einleuchtend, daß eben die lebenswichtigsten Beziehungen der menschlichen Existenz in ihren allgemeinen Formen besonders dazu geeignet sind, in der grammatischen Form (als Bedeutungsgehalt dieser Form) fixiert zu werden. Und die allgemeinsten lebenswichtiegen Beziehungen müssen ja für die verschiedensten Völker, besonders wenn sie auf gleicher Entwicklungestufe stehen, aber zum Teil sogar auch darüber hinaus, ungefähr die gleichen sein.

Es ist somit von vornherein anzunehmen, daß, wenn man zur Erforschung des Bedeutungsgehalts der grammatischen Formen einer unbekannten Sprache gelangt, sich darin gewisse grammatische Bedeutungen bei gewissen Formen geltend machen werden. Aber – und das möchte ich aufs entschiedenste betonen – eine derartise Annahme ist eben nur eine Annahme und darf nicht als eine sichere methodische Anleitung aufgefaßt werden. Die Möglichkeiten der Deduktion, die sich dabei ergeben, sind eben nur Möglichkeiten. Man soll sie gewiß ausnützen, aber sie dürfen nicht den induktiven Charakter der Analyse von grammatischen Bedeutungen verwischen, der bei der Erforschung des konkreten grammatischen Systems jeder Sprache vorherrschend sein soll. Denn es gibt keine automatische Verbindung von gewissen Bedeutungen mit gewissen grammatischen Formen. Die Bedeutung der grammatischen Formen ist, wie ich bereits gezeigt habe, ein kompliziert strukturiertes System, das sich in jeder Sprache auf verschiedene Weise gestaltet und sich dabei beständig verändert.

Eben deswegen haben, wie ich bereits gesagt habe, alle grammatisch-semantischen Systeme, die aufgestellt werden, im Grunde genommen nur als systematisierte Listen der tatsächlich vorkommenden grammatischen Bedeutungen zu gelten. Und meine Behauptung, daß diese Listen auf induktivem Wege erarbeitet werden sollen, läßt sich somit nicht völlig aufheben, sondern nur beschränken. Es ist nämlich bei solcher Prozedur auch ein deduktives Verfahren möglich und sogar notwendig, aber nur in gewissen Grenzen. Sowohl rein induktive, als auch rein deduktive Verfahrensweisen sind ja überhaupt in der Wissenschaft unmöglich – selbst in der scheinbar rein deuktiven Mathematik, wo die Axiomatik letzten Endes induktiven Ursprungs ist. Aber als Hauptsache bei der Ergründung der Bedeutung von grammatischen Formen einer konkreten Sprache bleibt doch das induktive, empirish-analytische Verfahren.

Deswegen bedeutet jeglicher Versuch, die systemarisierten Thesauren der grammatischen Bedeutungen als besondere grammatisch-semantische Systeme darzustellen, die ihre eigene Existenz haben und die semantische Grundlage und Voraussetzung der konkreten grammatischen Formen bilden, eine Verletzung der tatsächlichen Struktur des grammatischen Baus der Sprache und seiner semantischen Struktur. Dies gilt für alle semantischen Systeme, die aufgrund der für die Generativistik in allen ihren Ausrichtungen kennzeichnenden prinzipiellen Trennung von syntaktischer und semantischer Komponente, d.h. von Syntax und Semantik vorgeschlagen wurden. Die dabei aufgestellten Systeme von Tiefenstrukturen, semantischen Modellen usw. sind als selbständige Systeme rein semantischer, semiotischer Natur und stehen somit außerhalb der Grammatik. Und als solche sind sie gewiß zulässig und für irgendwelche semiotische Zwecke sogar sehr brauchbar. Aber für die Erkenntnis der konkreten grammatischen Formen einer konkreten Sprache sind solche verabsolutierte semantische Systeme als solche wertlos, sogar gefährlich, da sie, wie gesagt, bei ihrer konsequenten Durchführung die konkreten grammatischen Formen zu rein formalen asemantischen Gebilden degradieren, zu den Oberflächenstrukturen, die ihre Semantik als diskrete Bedeutung von den Tiefenstrukturen erhalten und syntaktisch den asemantischen Regeln der Dependenzgrammatik unterworfen sind. Dies alles steht in krassem Widerspruch zu dem tatsächlich existierenden System der Bedeutungen von grammatischen Formen, das ich oben entworfen habe und das durch die Feldstruktur dieser Formen, durch ihre sich stets verlagernden syntaktisch-semantischen Projektionen oder Perspektiven[15], durch ihre batysmatische Uberlagerung von verschiedenen grammatischen Bedeutungen (besonders im Redestrom) gekennzeichnet ist.

In Wirklichkeit sind dabei solche verabsolutisierts semantische Systeme der Tiefenstrukturen usw. in der Regel immer – bewußt oder unbewußt – aufgrund von tatsächlich existierenden Bedeutungen der grammatischen Formen in einer Sprache (oder einigen Sprachen) aufgestellt worden. Es kanna ja auch nicht anders sein. Denn die Zahl der Erscheinungsformen der objektiven Welt, der Beziehungsarten zwischen den Gegenständen und ihren Merkmalen ist ja unüberschaubar. Und in verschiedenen Sprachen, die verschedenen Bau aufweisen und auf verschiedenen Entwicklungsstufen stehen, treten sehr verschiedene Arten solcher Erscheinungsformen und Beziehungen als verallgemeinerte Bedeutungen von grammatischen Formen auf. So sollte es beim Versuch, ein für alle Sprachen gültiges System der Tiefenstrukturen aufzustellen, letzten Endes dazu kommen, daß im Prinzip die ganze Mannigfaltigkeit der Erscheinungsformen und Beziehungen der objektiven Welt in das System der Tiefenstrukturen usw aufgenommen werden sollte. Aber dies würde ja eben den rein semiotischen, außergrammatischen Status des Systems von Tiefenstrukturen usw. unwildersprechlich bestätigen. Doch so weit ist es selbstverständlich noch nicht gekommen.

Es bleibt also dabei, daß die generativistischen Systeme der Tiefenstrukturen usw. in Wahrheit nur Hilfsmittel sind, den Bedeutungsgehalt der grammatischen Formen in einer Sprache (oder in einigen Sprachen) zu systematisieren. Sobald sie den Anspruch erheben, als eine reelle und dabei entscheidende Macht in dem Bereich der Grammatik aufzutreten, als das eigentliche System der grammatischen Semantik, erweisen sie sich als fiktive Gebilde, die der Grammatik als Wissenschaft im Ganzen schädlich sind. Dementsprechend ist jeder Versuch der Generativistik, sich zu verabsolutieren und als Ersatz für alle anderen Grammatiktheorien aufzutreten, eine unbegründete Anmaßung, die unbedingt zu verwerfen ist.

Man hat auch zu berücksichtigen, daß die semantischen Termini, die in den generativistischen Theorien verwendet werden, oft einander widersprechen und in vielen Fällen schwer zu akzeptieren sind. So scheint der Begriff 'Situation', der häufig als die Bedeutung gilt, die die Tiefenstruktur des Satzes ausmacht, wenig passend, da der semantische Gehalt der Sätze mit dem Adjektivprädikativ oder dem nominativischen Substntivprädikativ sich nur auf künstliche Weise als 'Situation' darstellen läßt. Ich halte auch jetzt an der Meinung fest, daß der Bedeutungsgehalt des Satzes sich in allgemeinster Form als 'Beziehung' umschreiben läßt.[16]

Aber als Hilfsmittel, als Systematisierung der induktiv gewonnenen Ergebnisse der Analyse von Bedeutungen der grammatischen Formen sind solche semantische Thesauren, wie sie die Generativistik handhabt, und die Transformationen, die dabei verwendet werden, zum Teil von großem Nutzen.

Sie erleichtern die Arbeit an den kontrastiven Grammatiken, sind unentbehrlich bei der Ausarbeitung der – übrigens in der Regel durchaus problematischen – Universalien. Vom Standpunkt der Geschichte der Sprachwissenschaft bietet die Generativistik (dank ihrer betont scientifistischen Form) manchen Forschern eine bequeme methodische

Gelegenheit, von dem antimentalistischen Deskriptivismus zu einer solchen Grammatiktheorie überzugehen, die die Semantik in ihre Analyse miteinbezieht. Und vor allem bringt, wie gesagt, eine systematische Handhabung der Bedeutungen von grammatischen Formen große Vorteile, selbst in terminologischer Sicht. Sie erlaubt leichter und präziser die sich auf verschiedene Weise einander überlagernden Bedeutungen verschiedener grammatischer Formen miteinander zu vergleichen und in angemessenen Fällen zu identifizieren.

Es darf somit keine Rede sein von der völligen Ausschaltung der generativistisch-transformationallen Methodik aus dem Bereich der grammatischen Zugriffe. Es wurden ja auch bekanntlich die Transformationen seit langem in der grammatischen Forschung angewandt. Aber es soll sich dabei eben um *eine* von verschiedenen Methodiken und methodischen Zugriffen der grammatischen Theorie handeln, und das System von Tiefenstrukturen usw. soll nur als eine systematisierte Liste von verallgemeinerten grammatischen Bedeutungen der grammatischen Formen gelten, also als eine Hilfsoperation bei der Aufstellung des wirklichen Systems der grammatischen Bedeutungen einer konkreten Sprache. Und dieses System erweist sich als eine komplizierte multidimensionale Struktur die sich aus der Wechselwirkung der an die grammatischen Formen gebundenen verschiedenartigen grammatischen Bedeutungen ergibt, die selbst auf komplizierte Weise als semantische Feldstrukturen auftreten.[17]

ANMERKUNGEN

1 Vgl. S. Karcevsky, *Du dualisme asymmétrique du signe linguistique*, TCLP, I, 1929.

2 Z. B. Sütterlin, *Neuhochdeutsche Grammatik* (München, 1924), S. 317.

3 Vgl. W. G. Admoni, *Grundlagen der Grammatiktheorie*, aus dem Russischen übersetzt und mit einem Vorwort von Dr. Th. Lewandowski (Heidelberg, 1971), S. 26–27, 30ff. Spezieller über diese Problematik s. in meine Aufsätzen: 'Der Bedeutungsgehalt der grammatischen Formen im Sprachunterricht', in *Sprachwissenschaft und Sprachdidaktik*, Sprache der Gegenwart, Bd.XXXVI (Düsseldorf, 1975), 'Status obobščennogo grammatičeskogo značenija v sisteme jazyka', in *Voprosy jazykoznanija* (1975), Nr. 1.

4 Vgl. V. G. Admoni, 'Status obobščennogo grammatičeskogo značeni-ja. . .', S. 44–45.

5 Vgl. W. G. Admoni, 'Satzmodelle und logisch-grammatische Satzty-pen', in *Deutsch als Fremdsprache* (1974), H. 1; V. G. Admoni. 'Obladajut li modeli predlozenija obobscennym grammatičeskim značenijem?', in *Grammatičeskije issledovanija* (Leningrad, 1975).

6 Vgl. *Grundlagen der Grammatiktheorie*, S. 68–73.

7 Vgl. W. G. Admoni, *Der deutsche Sprachbau*, 3. Aufl. (München, 1970), S. 235–239.

8 Über die logisch-grammatischen und kommunikativ-grammatischen Kategorien vgl. *Der deutsche Sprachbau*, S. 5–6.

[9] Es handelt sich dabei auch um eine Art von Feldern semantisch-lexikal-grammatischer Art. Vgl. den Begriff 'Modalfeld' bei H. Brinkmann, *Die deutsche Sprache. Gestalt und Leistung* (Düsseldorf, 1962), S. 359ff. E. V. Gulyga und F. I. Šendels, *Grammatiko-leksič*eskije polja v sovremennon nemeckom jazyke (Moskva, 1969). A. V. Bondarko, 'K problematike funkcionalno-semanticeskich kategorij', in *Voprosy jazykoznanja* (1967), H. 2.

[10] Über den multidimensionalen Status der grammatischen Erscheinungen überhaupt vgl. *Grundlagen der Grammatiktheorie*, S. 54–68.

[11] Vgl. *Der deutsche Sprachbau*, S. 248–253.

[12] Vgl. *Der deutsche Sprachbau*, S. 254.

[13] S. V. G. Admoni, 'Partiturnoje strojenije rečevoj cepi i sistema grammatičeskich značenij v predloženii', in *Filologičeskije nauki* (1961), Nr. 3. Vgl. auch: *Grundlagen der Grammatiktheorie*, S. 59–68. Das in dem letzgenannten Buch angeführte Beispiel der Mehrschichtigkeit der grammatischen Bedeutungen in der Redekette (die 'Kolonne' der grammatischen Bedeutungen auf der Wortform 'Hunde' im Satz 'Die Hunde bellen') sollte eigentlich noch um die grammatische Bedeutung des Nominativs vermehrt werden, so daß die Gesamtzahl der auf der Wortform 'Hunde' direkt oder indirekt ruhended grammatischen Bedeutungen bis auf 12 steigen sollte.

[14] V. Admoni, 'Struktura predloženija', in *Voprosy nemeckoj grammatiki v istoričeskom osveščenii* (Leningrad, 1935), S.6. Die deutsche Ubersetzung dieses Aufsatzes ('Die Struktur des Satzes', in *Das Ringen um eine neue deutsche Grammatik*, Darmstadt, 1962) ist wegen Raummangel in gekürzter Form erschienen, so daß in ihr die betreffende Stelle fehlt.

[15] Ich gebe hier keine nähere Erklärung des außerordentlich wichtigen Begriffs der semantisch-syntaktischen Projektion (oder Perspektive), da ich vor kurzem dieses Problem an einem konkreten Beispiel ausführlich behandelt habe. S. den Aufsatz 'Es handelt sich um "es" ', in *Wirkendes Wort*, 1976, H. 4. Vgl. auch H. Brinkmann, 'Die "haben" – Perspektive im Deutschen', in *Sprache – Schlüssel der Welt*, Festschrift für Leo Weisgerber (Düsseldorf, 1959).

[16] Vgl. W. Admoni, 'Die Struktur des Satzes', in *Das Ringen um eine neue deutsche Grammatik*, hsg. v. H. Moser (Darmstadt, 1962), S. 387.

[17] Es gibt mehrere Klassifikationen von lexikalen und grammatischen Bedeutungen, die die terminologische Scheidung von solchen Komponenten der lexikalen und grammatischen Semantik einführen möchten wie 'Bedeutung', 'Bezeichnung', 'Sinn', 'kategoriale Semantik' usw. Ich begnüge mich mit dem Hinweis auf die eben erschienene, allerdings unmittelbar nur auf die lexikale Semantik ausgerichtete scharfsinnige Untersuchung von E. Coseriu, 'Die funktionelle Betrachtung des Wortschatzes' (in *Probleme der Lexikologie und Lexikographie*, Sprache der Gegenwart, Bd. XXXIX, Düsseldorf, 1976). Doch glaube ich, daß die von mir vorgeschlagene Analyse des Bedeutungsgehalts der grammatischen Formen die die Strukturiertheit dieser Formen in ihrer ganzen konkreten Kompliziertheit zum Vorschein bringt, es erlaubt, ohne solche terminologische Trennung verschiedener Seiten des grammatischen Bedeutungsgehalts auszukommen, da solche Trennung doch auch grundsätzliche Verschiedenheit im Wesen der betreffenden Erscheinungen voraussetzt. In Wirklichkeit aber, wie ich zu zeigen versuchte, sind dies alles nur mannigfaltige, variierende, in verschiedenem Grade verallgemeinerte, funktionell verschiedenartig ausgerichtete, einander überlagernde und sich kreuzende Abstufungen, Brechungen und Abwandlungen eines und desselben

Elements von Begriffen und Bedeutungen, die gedanklich – wiederum in verschiedenen Brechungen – die Erscheinungen und Beziehungen der gesamten Welt erfassen und somit alle als Bedeutungen zu werten sind. Diese Bedeutungen können sehr verschiedener Art sein, was auch terminologisch zum Ausdruck in diesem Aufsatz gebracht wurde, aber sie bleiben doch letzten Endes eben die den grammatischen Formen innewohnenden Bedeutungen und bilden in jeder Sprache ein sehr kompliziertes und asymmetrisches, aber doch einheitliches System.

A. NAESS

THE EMPIRICAL SEMANTICS OF KEY TERMS, PHRASES AND SENTENCES

EMPIRICAL SEMANTICS APPLIED TO NON-PROFESSIONAL LANGUAGE

1. Characterization of Empirical Semantics Through Contrasts

In what follows I will not discuss every sort of empirical semantics, but a kind or trend that has been given the proper name Empirical Semantics and has mainly flourished in Scandinavia. Its characteristics are most easily grasped by contrasting it with other trends.

If carried out with an open mind, painstaking empirical research leads us into vast uncharted regions of facts and relations. The more one penetrates the thickness of such regions, the more one is fascinated. One is – often against one's will – drawn further and further into the study of details and intricate structures revealed by the data found or collected. Bystanders are often astonished at this: What has gradually broadened into a whole world is, seen from outside, only a secondary and special field or at least a field of no importance for any great problems. And the outsider is right: it is only very rarely that a piece of empirical research obtains a great weight in solving or clarifying central problems. For example: Increase of status of particulars since the start (about 1962) of the international ecological movement: (1) Study of the *particular* habits of *particular* insects, (2) Study of the effects of putting 100 new chemicals into the environment through the study of the astronomical number of particular effects resulting from the combined action and interaction of 2, 3, 4, . . . 100 of those chemicals.

In contrast to the logical empiricism of the middle thirties Empirical Semantics stresses the requirement of testability of every direct and implied hypothesis about the actual use of terms, phrases or sentences. An instance: Alfred Tarski's work on truth included assertions about the agreement of his truth-definition or construction with the ordinary or common use of the term. But the testability of those assertions were low and there was no methodology agreed upon how to test them. The assessment of credibility was left to a kind of intuition believed to be more or less infallible among persons speaking the language. Logical

S. Kanger and S. Öhman (eds.), Philosophy and Grammar, 135–154.

empiricists, except Otto Neurath, accepted Tarski's assertions about the use of true and truth, and of many other terms without questioning them. In this they were of course not alone, but it contrasted with their very high level of requirement of testability and derivability in natural sciences, primarily in physics. Their methodology had a kind of blind spot in the matter of actual use of terms. Empirical Semantics stepped in and offered to clarify the limits of the adequacy of the Tarski definition, using testable methods.

Karl Popper, and later Paul Feyerabend and others trained by Popper, were here in agreement with logical empiricists, but tended to avoid semantical hypotheses. Popper certainly relied upon them indirectly, i.e. in assertions about induction. If this term is not used in certain ways which are only representing a subclass of the usages of the term, the thesis that good scientists never apply induction certainly falls to the ground. The same holds about what he says about metaphysics.

Late in the thirties, logical empiricists cooperated with Charles W. Morris and introduced the triad syntactical, semantical and pragmatic questions in dealing with language. The approach in pragmatics was called empirical, but it lacked a research methodology. Empirical assertion of grave importance in syntactical and semantical work was still left unsupported and relied upon an implicit appeal to intuition. Such appeals are of course unavoidable in more than 99% of our discussions, but of little weight when we face disagreements about usage which affect the arguments for or against a thesis of interest.

Belief in intuition corroborated by highly sophisticated arguments also characterized the Ordinary Language movement. J. L. Austin, Norman Malcolm and Herman Tennessen argued about the grammatical principle 'no modification without aberration', concentrating on phrases like 'I yawned voluntarily (or deliberately)' which Austin held to be 'impossible' under certain circumstnaces. Tennessen maintained a 'principle of tolerance' based on empirical semantical investigations. Tennessen contended that the intuitions of Austin concerning adverbs were deductions from old-fashioned grammar. He confirmed his own views through comparison with yawning students of which he found a great number in university reading rooms. When Feyerabend states that for 'years Lakatos and I were alone in our attempt to inject a little life, some personal note into philosophical debate', he forgets Tennessen. (*J. Br. Ph. Sc.*, 1976, p. 381.)

The highly intelligent and sophisticated assertions of Strawson about the performative function of sentences like 'It is true' can only be tested in concrete life situations. It is my contention that if we as researchers in such situations asked ordinary people about the purpose or meaning or job of such a sentence, they would in much less clever, but clearer, phrases outline different performative and non-performative functions. Lacking doctrinal prejudices, they avoided many pitfalls.

This example brings me to a second main tendency within Empirical Semantics: The relativity high regard for hypotheses put forth by non-professional philosophers concerning language.

An investigation of the use of the term 'true' and related terms such as 'fact' and 'probable' turned in the thirties to the question of how non-professional philosophers would themselves conceive the meaning and function of these words.

Philosophers have ready-made answers both to the use and the conception of the use among people outside their clan. I quote some phrases they use:

"The opinion of the man in the street on the truth-notion is . . .", "To naive people truth means . . .", "The usual criterion of error is . . .", "Wenn man einen Bauer fragen wollte, warum er glaube, dass. . .", "Die sinnliche Wahrheit ist die Wahrheit des Kindes", "Das Volk, als solches, oder der grosse Haufen, ist an seinen Vorstellungen an die Wahrheit der Sinne gebunden", "Der Character des Volkes und seiner Wahrheit ist Realismus", ". . .the definition of the truth and falsity of beliefs is not quite as simple as common-sense and MacTaggart suppose", "If common-sense had been asked to formulate what is meant by the truth of a belief, this is probably what it would have written. . .", ". . .Dies liegt in dem blossen Sinn der Worte wahr und falsch", "'Wahr' (in der üblichen Bedeutung) ist. . .", "Die Wahrheit ist, wie es scheint, von allen Menschen als etwas Festes, als etwas Unveränderliches und Ewiges, angesehen".

The quotations indicate a grave underestimation of non-philosophers, especially in regard to the diversity of 'embryonic' philosophical theories among non-professionals.

Asked (roughly) what is common to all that is true, people who have never read any philosophical papers or conversed with philosophers answer with formulations that have been put into more than 30 classes. Class No. 8 we might call the Tarski-class. What is true is identified with what is the case, what is so, or its function is conceived as a mere repetition of an assertion. The most frequent kind of formulation, class

10, identifies what is true with what is shown, or what is proved. It might be called the verification class.

Logicians trespassing in empirical semantics have objected to the truth-verification notions saying that 'not true' is clearly not synonymous with 'not verified'. But non-philosophers defend their notion maintaining synonymity hypotheses like the following:

(1) '*p* is true' syn '*p* is verified'
'*p* is not true' syn '*p* is falsified'

(2) 'it is not true that *p* is true' syn 'it is falsified that *p* is verified'

From (1) and (2) it does not follow

(3) 'true' syn 'verified'
'not true' syn 'not verified'

I shall of course not try to defend every non-philosopher's view, but only suggest that they are closely similar to a variety of professional views. The consistency of their views and terminologies tends to be underrated.

Philosophers mostly think that 'agreement with reality' is the common-sense conception. Formulations including references to reality, real things, etc. are put in class 1 in the above mentioned systems, and represent the fifth most frequent way of answering the question.

The non-professional's formulations describing criteria or giving definitions of 'what is true' may of course be classified in many ways. Above I have referred to a 'class 1'. In the same classification formulations are put into:

group 4 if truth is identified (in various senses) with a relation of correspondence with facts or actual things;

group 7 if truth is identified with facts or real things;

group 8 if truth is identified with what is the case, what is so, what is as one says. Furthermore, when a function of mere affirmation is described. Cf. the answers of person B to the utterance of A: A – It is raining, B – (1) Yes it is raining, (2) It is raining, (3) That is so, (4) Yes. ('The Tarski Group');

group 9 if what is true is identified with something fixed and determined by man himself ('Truth as Convention');

group 11 if what is true is identified with what cannot be challenged, disproved, contradicted, discussed or with what is indisputable;

group 12 if what is true is identified with what is unchangeable or what cannot be otherwise. Central notion: changelessness ('The Parmenides Group');

group 13 if what is true is identified with the relation of agreement or correspondence between something and *observation*;

group 14 if what is true is identified with something unmistakeable, with something that *cannot be mistaken*. ('Incorrigibility Group');

group 15 if what is true is identified with that which cannot be *doubted* or with what is not actually doubted by anyone. ('The Cartesian Group'.)

Sometimes the formulations are put forth with a low degree of definiteness of intention, but occasionally further conversation reveals astonishing consistency.

Empirical investigations suggest that *a large variety of philosophical outlooks* are alive among non-professionals in a potential, implicit or 'embryonic' form. One-sided education in colleges and universities perhaps reduces this diversity and works towards grey uniformity or excessive reliance upon the experts of the day.

But let me add some words to the characterization of Empirical Semantics through contrasts.

Empirical Semantics is heavily influenced by Bronislaw Malinowski and the linguists who since the late 19th century fought the 'intellectualist' conception of language as expression of thought. In a supplement to Ogden and Richards' provocative work *The Meaning of Meaning* Bronislaw Malinowski pointed to basic functions of language in situations of fishing, hunting, and other relations studied by social anthropology and now, also by modern etiology. Malinowski's conception and methodology contrasted markedly with the model of language as a calculus or as a set of rules for true/false assessments, and with the early Wittgenstein. In Vienna Carl Bühler was active in propagating a much broader and more empirical-minded view of language. When the later Wittgenstein proposed a more empirical and etiological view, this was greeted in circles of Empirical Semantics with sincere appreciation, but it did not seem to convey more or clearer information than the old social anthropology of language. The tumultuous applause accorded to Wittgenstein's non-intellectual view of language seems to have had as a necessary condition the insularity of Anglo-American philosophical centres in matters of social science.

In the forties social science was able to sweep into European and Anglo-American universities on a grand scale. A highly critical, if not contemptuous, attitude towards the newcomer was, however, prevalent in philosophical environments. Logical empiricists tended to talk about social scientists, including psychologists, as hard working, not too sharp fellows, who did not really know what they were doing. With some patience, this could, however, be shown them through logical analysis of the sentences they produced.

At the very bottom of the social science methodological status ladder we find the questionnaire, perhaps best known among philosophers from semi-commercial undertakings and Gallup surveys.

From the very beginning questionnaires have been extensively used in Empirical Semantics. Their usefulness or even unavoidableness is rather obvious if uses of a sentence among a large group of users are to be tested in an interpersonally satisfactory way.

Example: In a small room with a globe near the subject, he or she will very often use the sentence 'The earth is round' if asked to give an example of something true. The example is convenient for introducing questions about the certainty that the earth is round, possibilities of errors, questions of preciseness when compared to formulations in terms of a mathematical sphere and of more complex forms. In more or less 'open interviews' a 'common characteristic of truth' question could then be introduced under standardized conditions. Non-standardized conditions involve too many variables.

2. *Rules or Habits*

The kind of research programmes which in the forties got the label Empirical Semantics must be understood as in part a strong reaction against uncritical applications of the conception of a language as a system of rules. The distinction of de Saussure between *parole* and *language* is fruitful to a point, but can be overdone. E.S. also reacted against the position that many of the classical problems of philosophy could be clarified – or even solved – through transforming them from ontological and epistemological questions to questions of language and of choice of sets of rules.

The limited force of rules may be understood from the fact that no set of rules, however comprehensive and however precise, can unambiguously determine relevant behaviour patterns of an action. This holds, for instance, for an action of the kind called 'testing the hypothesis *H* through method *M*'. What is indicated through rules is primarily traits of behaviour which *seem to be in need of being indicated*, given certain habits or mores of the community *at the time of* making the rule and in its social and physical context. Whether we do research or fish with the help of big nets, and try to describe our doings, there always *remain* relevant undescribed traits. The 'outsider', if sufficiently distant culturally, cannot use the description, whatever the quality of the translation.

3. *Main Fields of Research in Empirical Semantics*

The E.S. investigations have centred upon a fairly small number of topics:

(1) *Occurrence Analysis*. Description of function or connotations of certain key terms based on analysis of large numbers of occurrences of the terms in definite texts. Of occurrence analysis there are several sorts.

(2) *Metaoccurrence Analysis*. (a) Synchronic description of definitions and other metaoccurrences and their relation to occurrences. Among other data, 500 definitions of truth by non-professional and scores of definitions by professional philosophers were analyzed. (b) Metaoccurrence Analysis as part of historical research. E.g. metaoccurrences of 'democracy' from the French to the Russian Revolutions.

(3) *Agreement and Disagreement Analysis*. Example: Assessment of the scope and function of pseudoagreement and pseudodisagreement in scientific argumentations and ideological disputes.

(4) *Definiteness of Intention Analysis*. The definiteness of intended meaning is always limited, or in other terms, the net of discriminations relative to things (not constructs, like π) has a limited finiteness. There are ways to discover the limits, assess their function, and if desirable for certain purposes, increase the definiteness or depth of intention.

(5) *Synonymity*, or more generally, equivalence and analyticity analysis. Elaboration of tests of criteria of close similarity of meaning, or more generally, of function. Estimation of degree of analyticity in communication. Whereas there may be doubt about certain analyticity concepts, the fruitfulness of the empirical kind has already been confirmed.

(6) Contributions to theory of communication and to the development of educational instruments in favour of more effective cognitive communication. These contributions furnish the conceptual framework of the above mentioned researches.

In close connexion with E.S. there are efforts to elicit 'embryonic' philosophies of truth and related topics among non-philosophers, and of logical calculi like propositional calculi, and of probability. As a curiosity may be mentioned that the frequencies of unlikely series, for instance, to get 6 heads when tossing a coin 6 times, are markedly underrated if we permit ourselves to take the internationally established statistics to be correct. Such statistics have been extensively verified, but established propositional calculus should *not* be taken as an absolute. Here I disagree with Piaget who in his experiments and interpretations takes established logic and physics at face value.

4. *Synonymity, Operations and Operationism*

A. *Pseudoagreement Analysis*

The synonymity research within E.S. reveals heavy stress on operational definitions, as part of the requirements of interpersonal testability, but emphatic rejection of operationism (á la Bridgman or in modern forms). The rejection is a clear consequence of the semantics of preciseness and the rejection of 'correct meaning': With 'intelligence' as a T_0, one may expect an indefinite multiplicity of plausible synonymic alternatives of different orders of preciseness. To choose one and act as if it were the only one is a form of linguistic corruption. Furthermore, fruitful operational definitions are mostly transintentional or they are technifications rather than precizations. The designation 'definition' is misleading.

The positive attitude towards interpersonal explicitly described operations and the negative towards operationism is part of a general attitude within epistemology or semantics: that of unending, expanding research rather than of science. At no point are there decisive conclusions. Research programmes are closed for practical reasons, not for cognitive.

For instance, agreement and disagreement are never free of possible mixture of pseudoagreement and pseudodisagreement. The research on, e.g., agreement on definitions or precizations of the term 'democracy', are in E.S. steered in such a way that no tests are taken to be conclusive. There are only instances of confirmations and disconfirmations, the weight of which cannot be exactly assessed.

The conceptual framework of E.S. is simple in its essentials:

Basic predicate:

(1) Syn (*xyz*, *tuv*)

'*x* is synonymous for *y* in situation *z* with *t* for *u* in *v*'.

x is said to be synonymic alternative (more loosely: 'interpretation') of *t*, and *t* of *x*.

Situations are in (1) considered to be singular, dated situations.

Three special cases of (1):

(2) (*y*)(*u*) Syn (*xyz*, *tuv*)

'for all persons is *x* in situation *z* synonymous with *t* in situation *v*'.

(3) (*z*)(*v*) Syn (*xyz*, *tuv*)

'in all situations is *x* for *y* synonymous with *t* for *u*'.

(4) Syn (*xyz*, *tyv*)

'*x* for *y* in *z* is synonymous with *t* for *y* in *v*'.

Synonymity is not defined, but a variety of operational definitions or technifications, are introduced, such as substitutability of *x* with *t*.

On the basis of synonymity a number of other concepts are introduced: precization, definition, pseudoagreement and pseudodisagreement, analyticity, biased interpretation, popularization,. . .

Precization is contrasted with specification and elaboration.

B. Experiment on Definiteness of Intention

One may struggle to find suitable words for a thought or feeling, but one may also struggle to find out what was meant by an utterance. The utterance may have had the form of an assertion, it may belong to accepted hypothesis within a science, but this does not solve the problem what a particular person in a particular situation intended to express by the assertive sentence, or what it conveyed to listeners.

In order to investigate the latter, certain experiments were performed by empirical semanticists. I shall give one example: The experimenter announced a lecture to an association of students of physics, and about 250 gathered in an auditorium. After talking for about 20 minutes the lecturer said: 'The earth is surrounded by a gravitational field' in a rather natural context, but without particular stress. This was a signal to a mob of assistants to invade the gathering with copies of a questionnaire which were handed to the students. The basic question read: "How did you interpret the utterance 'The earth is surrounded by a gravitational field?'" "Do any of the following sentences convey to you what the utterance conveyed to you?"

Two classes of answers are of particular interest, the 'I do not know'-answers and the 'no discrimination' answers. They reveal the limits of the definiteness of interpretation among hearers.

C. *Are Tarski's empirical hypotheses testable*?

The clash of opinions on language was clearly shown behind the scenes of the Third Congress of Unity of Science in the Salle Descartes at the Sorbonne. What was Tarski really trying to do in his masterly dissertation on truth? Generally it was thus conceived:

> The task which Tarski sets for himself is that of finding a materially adequate and formally correct definition of truth. The requirement of material adequacy is *simply* the requirement that the definition, once achieved, shall correspond more or less closely with that concept of truth which all of us have in mind before we ever undertake the task of explication.[1]

The important theory of Tarski on truth, rescuing the objective or absolute concept of truth from relativism and subjectivism, was at the congress to be defended and duly hailed by Karl Popper.

I had a discussion note in which I maintained the following theses (here given in abbreviated form):

(1) The theory of Tarski contained empirical hypotheses: namely statements about ordinary language (*die Umgangssprache*).

(2) The statements are vague and ambiguous and not directly testable by research.

(3) Testability implies operationalization: the finding and communication of some procedures that can corroborate the modified hypotheses.

(4) Preliminary tests by simple social science techniques involving questionnaires and occurrence analysis suggest that the adequacy of the Tarski analysis is very limited.

(5) The extremely high level of preciseness and logical rigour of the formal development in Tarski's work contrast dramatically with the sloppiness of the statements about ordinary language.

(6) Any movement using the epithet empirical as a positive key-term should instigate empirical research in case this is necessary to confirm or disconfirm basic theories.

(7) The term 'true' is central in various fields of philosophy, and the suppression of certain directions of precization (that is, a subgroup of concepts) impairs or stultifies our minds. The claim that one concept is adequate favours dogmatism.

In the pre-conference before the opening of the session Carnap contended that the empirical material and the inferences drawn from it would cause confusion, not clarification. The objections by Neurath should suffice, and as they were well discussed beforehand, the plenum discussion would be fruitful and orderly. I agreed, having the feeling that nobody would think it even meaningful to do empirical *research* on ordinary language.

According to Tarski and those following him, the *Umgangssprache* permits unlimited (*unbeschränkt*) use of the concept of truth. Propositions which negate themselves are permitted.

Such a hypothesis is empirical and we must ask: how is it testable? By what procedures? How is the metaphor of 'permittance' eliminated? How are the rules of the *Umgangssprache* found?

The weight of the criticism of Tarski's hypothesis is not that it is false, but that it is not made operational and therefore not tested.

A kind of test was made in 1936 and the result was negative.[2] It made use of open questionnaires related to the antinomy of the liar. The persons speaking the *Umgangssprache* did not interpret any sentences in such a way that they negated themselves. The existence of a *rule* of the *Umgangssprache* that permits it were not in evidence, nor a *rule* that prohibits it. Rules may be *invented* which approximately picture the complex regularities of ordinary usage. In that case there will be no rule of unlimited use of 'true'.

D. *Analytic/Synthetic*

A kind of analytical/synthetical distinction is introduced in E.S., but not as an absolute distinction. The point of view of E.S. towards the debate on analytical/synthetical is best formulated in Åke Nordenstams' emminently clear dissertation, *Empiricism and the Analytic-Synthetic Distinction*.

Ludvig Løvestad, using E.S. procedures, concluded in 1945 that the analytic/synthetic distinction plays little or no role in natural science, and explained why. His work is little known, however.

It requires (1) sentences to be split into parts, and (2) the introduction of rules in relation to which sentences may be analytical or fall into a broader category of 'analytoform'. A sentence is analytoform if it for at least one plausible interpretation (synonymic alternative) is analytic.

A hypothesis that a sentence is analytical is confirmed only if it can be shown that it occurs within the context in which the rule is intended to be valid and only in relation to that rule. There may be a number of other rules (as in the case, e.g. of chemistry of acids) intended to cover the same or in part the same context. The same sentence may be non-analytic in relation to all rules except one. In most cases the task of interpretation of the rule formulation will not furnish any simple definite conclusion because of ambiguity and vagueness.

So much about the role of rules.

E. Translations

Under what condition would the sentence *U* be a *perfect translation* of the sentence *T*? The hunt for an eternally perfect translation for all people in all situations is rather pointless. As a point of departure we should, according to E.S., take particular acts of communication and ask for synonymity:

(1) $\text{Syn}\ (Up_1s_1;\ Tp_2s_2)$

where, e.g. s_1 is not a singular dated situation, but a *kind* of situation, for instance when using an implement for fishing (á la Malinowski). The person p_1 and p_2 may be considered to cooperate, in spite of having different mothertongues. Suppose after some time they use *T* or *U* as completely interchangeable in communication with each other *during fishing*. In other situations they may make a difference. We may introduce various tests or operational criteria of the interchangeability. On the basis of (1) the presence of two different mothertongues (*U* and not *T* belonging to one, and *T* and not *U* belonging to the other), and (2) the presence of certain kinds of synonymity operationally introduced through interpersonal test, we may define *U* as *a perfect translation* for p_1 and p_2 in s_1 and vice versa.

Generalizing, we may talk of the total class of persons p_1 speaking a certain language L_1 and the total class of persons p_2 speaking L_2. The chances of finding a perfect translation in this case, even if the kind of situation s_1 is very narrow, is, of course, very small. For most purposes translations very far from being perfect may do the job.

At this point measures of definiteness of intention are relevant. In general one may say that the chance of a perfect translation is

(1) inversely proportional to the degree of definiteness of intention required,

(2) proportional to the narrowness of class of persons,

(3) proportional to the narrowness of class of situations,

(4) inversely proportional to the distance between the two languages.

If we do not envisage a practical situation like fishing, but the translatability of an abstract text, e.g. one on democracy, occurrence and metaoccurrence analysis of a number of terms is required. The uses of the Russian term usually translated into Norwegian by the word 'demokrati', are obviously influenced by the happenings in Soviet Russia since 1917. The history of Norway has been quite different. Occurrence analysis today would reveal complicated differences. On the metalevel there are also differences. They may *in part* be roughly indicated by saying that economic relations between the citizens are in the Russian terminology highly relevant in estimating the degree to which a regime is democratic, whereas in Norwegian metaoccurrences references are mostly to elections and the structure of government in general.

In any case, meaning-hypotheses in the form of assertions saying that the term 'A' in language L_1 has the meaning B in the language L_2 can only be confirmed (or disconfirmed) to a certain degree. There will never be only one hypothesis that can *cover the total class of occurrences* within an interval of time. This is a situation commonly found in any empirical field of study. And, of course, there will be very different kinds of hypotheses in relation to the great variety of precizations of the world 'meaning'. In E.S. that term is avoided through use of the synonymity terminology. The above introduction of a term 'translation' indicated how the elimination is done in a particular case.

The above implies a thesis of 'indeterminacy of translation'. There are, e.g. indefinitely many rules (according to occurrence analysis) that in principle cover any set of occurrences of a term or sentence. Indefinitely many translations will all fit the occurrences. (But from this does not follow certain negative theorems recently formulated by D. Føllesdal.)

One persistent trait of E.S. is not only the equiminded acceptance of diversity of interpretations and hypotheses, but even the stress on listing diversities. The attitude is closely connected with attitudes in plant geography, social anthropology, local history, and other fields of 'soft' natural and humanist fields of research. It is very different from dominant attitudes in formal logic, mathematical physics and other 'tougher' fields. One may say that the extremely positive attitude toward diversity is in line with theorem 24 of part 5 of Spinoza's *Ethics*. 'The more we understand particular things the more we understand God'.

5. *'Showing' Contradictions*

This year – the tricentennial anniversary of his death – a great number of experts on Spinoza publish and lecture. Very few of them seem to believe in the fruitfulness of semantical studies. But the fruitfulness of E.S. occurrence analysis, and especially the equivalence analysis, seem to me to be beyond doubt in Spinoza research.

There are today still a number of experts on Spinoza who think they can *show* that Spinoza's Ethics contain contradictions in the sense of inconsistencies. In a recent lecture Leszek Kołakowski, before an audience of several hundred 'friends of Spinoza', announced a number of contradictions some of which he even contended he could *prove*. According to the methodology of occurrence analysis, it is impossible to *prove* such inconsistencies. Empirical working hypotheses cannot be proven. The methodological situation in this matter is not different from that in historical geology or in cosmology.

If we analyze the occurrences and metaoccurrences of basic terms of the Ethics, such as *liber* (free), *determinata* (determined), *potentia* (power), *virtus* (virtue), and others, a variety of interpretations are open. This holds even if we add information from other texts of Spinoza, and from authors with in part similar terminology, for instance Descartes. I shall later concentrate on one source of differences of interpretation, the expressions of equivalence.

If we have a pair sentences T_0 and U_0 which by superficial reading seem inconsistent, we might take this as a sufficient condition of inconsistency that for all pairs of plausible precizations beyond a certain level of preciseness, the pairs are instances of logical inconsistency. The judgment of plausibility is, however, highly speculative. There is no room for proofs in a rigorous or even a sloppy sense, there is only room for working hypotheses of limited testability. I say *working* hypotheses, because the assessment of plausibility of interpretation depends upon other sentences of the text which contain terms intimately connected with the term of T_0 and U_0. Thus research must proceed from a rather narrow set of terms or sentences to a very wide one. The sentences of the Ethics hang together, that we all agree upon.

The diversity of interpretations that fit the given class of occurrences of certain terms or sentences is best conceived if we think of them as interpretative rules. Using the broad theorem of Mach-Duhem-Poincaré in general methodology, we may say that there are indefinitely many different rules of grammar and dictionary consistent with a given set of occurrences of a term or sentence.

But let me mention a central term of Spinoza's Ethics, *liber*, free.

There is a famous absolutistic metaoccurrence of *res libera* (free thing) in Part 1 of the Ethics. A 'free thing' is by definition synonymous with 'a thing that exists solely out of the necessity of its own nature, and is determined to act solely out of itself'.

Every plausible interpretation of Spinoza's text at this point requires that we exclude human beings from the class of free things. Only one so-called thing is free, God, substance or Nature. Nevertheless Spinoza talks sometimes of the free human being, *homo liber*. If we accept the hypothesis that *liber* here is used in the same way as announced in his definition, we may infer that there not only are no *homo liber* but that the expression as it occurs in the Ethics involves a contradiction on the same shameless level as the famous 'square circle'.

But this conclusion leads to difficulties. According to the note on theorem 54 in Part 4, to live according to reason is to be free. (. . .*ex ductu rationis vivant, hoc est, ut liberi sint*.) The free human being seems to be, in Part 4, a being not determined to act solely out of itself, but to a high degree out of itself or from its own nature, or self-caused. Thus, Spinoza does not here exclude the possibility of free humans.

It cannot of course be proven, but a rather good hypothesis is the one that postulates an absolutistic and a non-absolutistic use of 'free' in Spinoza's texts. In other words, the term free is used in at least two senses. The absolutistic metaformulation might then be interpreted as synonymous with the more precise sentence: 'I am going to say (*dicetur*) that that thing is *absolutely* free, which exists *solely* out of the necessity of its own nature . . .'.

The talk about free human beings in the later parts of the Ethics will then naturally be interpreted in a non-absolute sense of 'free'. This approach is quite successful I think. It results in elimination of the threatening inconsistency when the metaoccurrence in part 1 is taken to cover all occurrences of 'free'. Every alleged inconsistency proclaimed by Kołakowski and by a number of other distinguished scholars can be eliminated in the same way. (This is strictly a working hypothesis.)

Every sentence announcing what *will be* said, using *futurum simplex*, implies, if the definiteness of intention is taken to be fairly high, an announcement of the range of intended validity. The Ethics consisted originally only of the first part, and the absolutistic use is confined to that. Consequently, we consider the intended range of validity to be limited to part 1.

Some experts think that Spinoza's *system* requires the absolute sense, but there is no way of getting to one single system as being that of Spinoza. What we can do is to introduce reconstructions, more or less freely. Personally I am for reconstructions that permit me to talk about human beings being able to obtain higher levels of freedom. That is being able to *increase* their level of freedom. This means that I prefer reconstructions such that the term 'free' is not used exclusively in an absolute sense.

In any case, neither the so-called determinism nor any other doctrine of the Ethics can be *shown* to contain inconsistencies. The methodology of occurrence analysis rules it out. A different methodology might be adopted, and in relation to that inconsistencies might be shown or even proved. No such methodology has been formulated by Spinoza experts, however.

Of more interest are attempts to interpret the Ethics in such a way that it becomes consistent from the point of view of formal logic. Professor J. Friedman has, in a not yet published dissertation, concluded that the proofs of Part 1 of the Ethics obtain a consistent and valid form if 164 premisses are added. This seems a somewhat big number, but all except about 20 are of a very innocent kind. The work is of interest for all who would wish to learn from Spinoza in a positive way.

6. *Expressions of Extensional Equivalence*

Nearness of cognitive meaning or function has always been a favourite theme of Empirical Semantics.

In the Ethics there are a number of expressions which suggest at least a kind of extensional or referential identity or near identity, in short, extensional equivalence with certain other expressions. Some pairs may be intensionally equivalent, but considering the nominalistic inclination of Spinoza, and also the difficulty in testing hypotheses of intension, I shall limit myself to extension.

Here are some of the expressions which consist of more than one word:

by *x* I understand *y* *per. . . intelligo. . .*
by *x* we understand *y* *per . . . intelligimus. . .*
to understand the same by *x* and *y* *per. . . et. . . idem intelligere*

x does not mean anything else than *y* . . .*nihil aliud significat quam*
x and *y* are one and the same . . .*unum et idem sunt*
x is nothing else than *y* . . .*nihil praeter. . . est*
x or (which is the same) *y* . . .*vel* (*quod idem est*). . .

Some of the others, consisting only of one or two words are very common. The most common is '*x* or *y*', *x sive y*, for instance 'God or Nature', *Deus sive Natura*. Other very common ones are '*x* or *y*' ('*x seu y*'), '*x*, that is, *y*' ('*x*, *hoc est, y*').

In all there are about 250 occurrences of expressions of extensional equivalence. Their exact interpretation is in most or all cases open to different views. The resulting differences in interpretation of the system of Spinoza are substantial. This is due to the fact that most of the fundamental terms of the system occur in equivalences.

An example: The terms 'power' and 'virtue' are connected with several strong terms of equivalence. There is also an equivalence between virtue and love of God. It is said in the proof of theorem 42 in Part 5 that love of God (*amor erga Deum*) is virtue itself (*ipsa virtus est*). Now, if in the Ethics we put the term 'virtue' wherever we find 'power' we get a text that sounds very Christian and very tender-minded in the sense of William

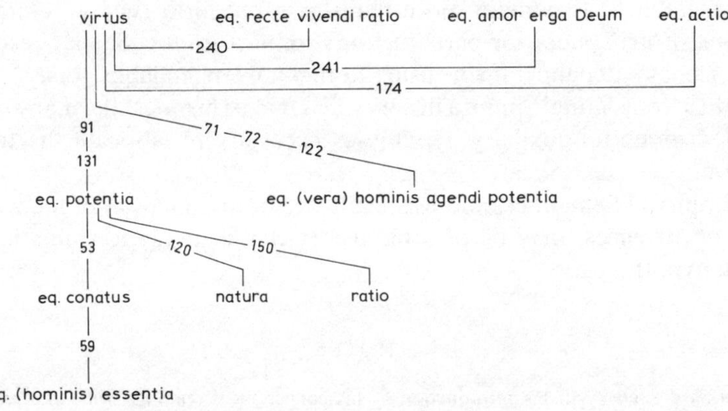

Fig. 1. Strings of equivalence: an example.[3] *Number references*: 53 – Part 3, Prop. 7, Demonstratio; 59 – Part 3, Prop. 9, Scholium; 71 – Part 3, Prop. 55, Scholium; 72 – Part 3, Prop. 55, Cor. 2, Dem.; 91 – Part 4, Def. 8; 120 – Part 4, Prop. 33, Dem.; 122 – Part 4, Prop. 52, Dem.; 150 – Part 4, App. 3; 174 – Part 5, Prop. 4, Scholium; 240 – Part 5, Prop. 41, Dem.; 241 – Part 5, Prop. 42, Dem.

James. If on the other hand we substitute 'power' everywhere for 'virtue', we get a text sounding of Machiavelli or Thomas Hobbes, and very tough-minded in the sense of William James.

Spinoza is said to be a *Gottbetrunkener Mensch*. This will be still more to the point if, where he writes 'virtue', we place 'love of God' instead. But since we have two famous equivalences of God and Nature, *Deus sive Natura*, we could, make a second choice, writing Nature wherever he has 'God'. He then suddenly changes from *ein Gottbetrunkener* to *ein Naturbetrunkener*, a kind of nature mystic.[4]

The semantical point to be made is that reconstructions must introduce a term or a complex expression that fits both *potentia* and *virtus*. Clearly neither the term 'power' nor the term 'virtue' can do the job. Or one might define completely new terms, for instance, '*potus*' or '*virtia*', analogous to Eddington's invitation to use 'waveicle' as a term in physics for an entity that in part has specific properties of waves, in part particles.

The important lesson is that the equivalences found in the Ethics rule out some interpretations of the basic terms as very implausible, but leave room for a number of very different others.

Basing our concept of interpretation upon the kind of concepts of synonymity suggested on p. 141, we may confidently predict that there will not be any convergence of interpretations of Spinoza's text with increase of research. It is perhaps more realistic to put forth general interpretations of his system, or parts of it, as *reconstructions*. Sender/receiver preciseness depends upon using terms understandable today. This implies 'translating' Spinoza in a way that makes manifest the many more or less doubtful auxiliary hypotheses necessary to fabricate the translation.

Empirical Semantics, and especially occurrence analysis of meta- and use-occurrences, may be of some use in clarification and validation of such hypotheses.

NOTES

[1] Leonard Lindsky in his introduction to his collection of readings *Semantics and the Philosophy of Language*, Univ. of Illinois Press, 1952. (My italics.)

[2] Referred to (shortly) on pp. 383–384 in *Erkenntnis*, Vol. 7.

[3] The numbers refer to the list of equivalences in A. Naess, *Equivalent Terms and Notions in Spinoza's Ethics*, *Inquiry*, University Press, Oslo, 1976.

[4] I do not take up the question of how 'strong' are the equivalences made use of in this example. Some are certainly too weak as basis for substitutability.

BIBLIOGRAPHY

In the following publications the authors, *inter alia*, explicitly make use of the kind of conceptual structure or of empirical procedure that are characteristic of Empirical Semantics.

Blom, Siri: 1955, 'Concerning a Controversy on the Meaning of Probability', *Theoria* **21**.

Christophersen, J. A.: 1967, *The Meaning of 'Democracy' as Used in European Ideologies from the French to the Russian Revolution*, Universitetsforlaget, Oslo.

Dahl, Ottar: 1956, *Om årsaksproblemer i historisk forskning*, Oslo.

Fløistad, G. and A. Naess: 1963–1964, *Spinoza's Etikk: Systematiske rekonstruksjoner*, I, II, III, Inst. of Philosophy, Oslo.

Gullvåg, I.: 1951, 'Definiteness of Intention', *Filosofiske Problemer*, No. 18.

Gullvåg, I.: 1954, 'Criteria of Meaning and Analysis of Usage', *Synthese* **9**.

Løvestad, L.L 1945, *Bidrag til en metodelaere for de eksakte naturvidenskaper, Filosofiske Problemer*, No. 3.

McKeon, R. (ed.): 1951, *Democracy in a World of Tensions*, University of Chicago Press.

Nordenstam, Åke: 1961, *Empiricism and the Analytic-Synthetic Distinction*, Gøteborg.

Naess, A. (also written Ness): 1938, 'Common-sense and Truth', *Theoria* **4**.

Naess, A.: 1938. *'Truth' as Conceived by Those Who Are Not Professional Philosophers*, Oslo.

Naess, A.: 1949, 'Toward a Theory of Interpretation and Preciseness', *Theoria* **15**, 220–241. Also in Lindsky, L. (ed.), *Semantics and the Philosophy of Language*, Univ. of Illinois Press, 1952.

Naess, A.: 1953, *Interpretation and Preciseness. A Contribution to the Theory of Communication. Det Norske viedenskapsakademi i Oslo, Skrifter, II, Hist.-filos.kl.*, 1953:1, Oslo, 1953.

Naess, A.: 1956, *Democracy, Ideology and Objectivity, Studies in the Semantics and Cognitive Analysis of Ideological Controversy*, ed. by Arne Naess, Jens A. Christophersen and Kiell Kyalø, Oslo.

Naess, A.: 1966, *Communication and Argument*, Elements of Applied Semantics, Transl. from the Norwegian by Alastair Hannay, Oslo.

Naess, A.: 1968, 'Demokratisk styreform', *Filosofiske Problemer*, No. 36, Mimeo.

Naess, A.: 19 , 'Logical Equivalence, Intentional Isomorphism and Synonymity as Studied by Questionnaires', *Synthese* **10**.

Naess, A.: 1975, *Freedom, Emotion and Selfsubsistence, The Structure of a Central Part of Spinoza's Ethics*, Oslo.

Ofstad, H.: 1950, 'The Descriptive Definition of the Concept "Legal Norm" as Proposed by Hans Kelsen', *Theoria* **16**.

Ofstad, H.: 1961, *An Inquiry into the Freedom of Decision*, Oslo.

Simonsson, T.: 1966, 'Begreppen 'tro'. En empirisk-semantisk studie', *Filosofiske Problemer*, No. 29.

Tejde, Jan Olav: 1966, 'Om värdetermer i religiöst språk', *Filosofiske Problemer*, No. 33.

Tennessen, H.: 1949a, '"Private Enterprise", A Semantical Study', in *The Psychological and Sociological Implications of Economic Planning in Norway*, Mimeo, Oslo.

Tennessen, H.: 1949b, 'Typebegreper I, II', *Filosofiske Problemer*, No. 12.

Tennessen, H.: 1959, 'What Should We Say?', *Inquiry* **2**.
Tennessen, H.: 1964, *Language Analysis and Empiricial Semantics, Eighteen Papers*, Univ. of Alberta.
Tennessen, H.: 1965, 'Ordinary Language *in memoriam*', *Inquiry* **8**.

INDEX OF SUBJECTS

SYNTHESE LIBRARY

Studies in Epistemology, Logic, Methodology,
and Philosophy of Science

1. J. M. Bochénski, *A Precis of Mathematical Logic.* 1959.
2. P. L. Guiraud, *Problèmes et méthodes de la statistique linguistique.* 1960.
3. Hans Freudenthal (ed.), *The Concept and the Role of the Model in Mathematics and Natural and Social Sciences.* 1961.
4. Evert W. Beth, *Formal Methods. An Introduction to Symbolic Logic and the Study of Effective Operations in Arithmetic and Logic.* 1962.
5. B. H. Kazemier and D. Vuysje (eds.), *Logic and Language. Studies Dedicated to Professor Rudolf Carnap on the Occasion of His Seventieth Birthday.* 1962.
6. Marx W. Wartofsky (ed.), *Proceedings of the Boston Colloquium for the Philosophy of Science 1961-1962.* Boston Studies in the Philosophy of Science, Volume I. 1963.
7. A. A. Zinov'ev, *Philosophical Problems of Many-Valued Logic.* 1963.
8. Georges Gurvitch, *The Spectrum of Social Time.* 1964.
9. Paul Lorenzen, *Formal Logic.* 1965.
10. Robert S. Cohen and Marx W. Wartofsky (eds.), *In Honor of Philipp Frank.* Boston Studies in the Philosophy of Science, Volume II. 1965.
11. Evert W. Beth, *Mathematical Thought. An Introduction to the Philosophy of Mathematics.* 1965.
12. Evert W. Beth and Jean Piaget, *Mathematical Epistemology and Psychology.* 1966.
13. Guido Küng, *Ontology and the Logistic Analysis of Language. An Enquiry into the Contemporary Views on Universals.* 1967.
14. Robert S. Cohen and Marx W. Wartofsky (eds.), *Proceedings of the Boston Colloquium for the Philosophy of Science 1964-1966. In Memory of Norwood Russell Hanson.* Boston Studies in the Philosophy of Science, Volume III. 1967.
15. C. D. Broad, *Induction, Probability, and Causation. Selected Papers.* 1968.
16. Günther Patzig, *Aristotle's Theory of the Syllogism. A Logical-Philosophical Study of Book A of the Prior Analytics.* 1968.
17. Nicholas Rescher, *Topics in Philosophical Logic.* 1968.
18. Robert S. Cohen and Marx W. Wartofsky (eds.), *Proceedings of the Boston Colloquium for the Philosophy of Science 1966-1968.* Boston Studies in the Philosophy of Science, Volume IV. 1969.

19. Robert S. Cohen and Marx W. Wartofsky (eds.), *Proceedings of the Boston Colloquium for the Philosophy of Science 1966-1968*. Boston Studies in the Philosophy of Science, Volume V. 1969.
20. J. W. Davis, D. J. Hockney, and W. K. Wilson (eds.), *Philosophical Logic*. 1969.
21. D. Davidson and J. Hintikka (eds.), *Words and Objections. Essays on the Work of W. V. Quine*. 1969.
22. Patrick Suppes, *Studies in the Methodology and Foundations of Science. Selected Papers from 1911 to 1969*. 1969.
23. Jaakko Hintikka, *Models for Modalities. Selected Essays*. 1969.
24. Nicholas Rescher *et al.* (eds.), *Essays in Honor of Carl G. Hempel. A Tribute on the Occasion of His Sixty-Fifth Birthday*. 1969.
25. P. V. Tavanec (ed.), *Problems of the Logic of Scientific Knowledge*. 1969.
26. Marshall Swain (ed.), *Induction, Acceptance, and Rational Belief*. 1970.
27. Robert S. Cohen and Raymond J. Seeger (eds.), *Ernst Mach: Physicist and Philosopher*. Boston Studies in the Philosophy of Science, Volume VI. 1970.
28. Jaakko Hintikka and Patrick Suppes, *Information and Inference*. 1970.
29. Karel Lambert, *Philosophical Problems in Logic. Some Recent Developments*. 1970.
30. Rolf A. Eberle, *Nominalistic Systems*. 1970.
31. Paul Weingartner and Gerhard Zecha (eds.), *Induction, Physics, and Ethics*. 1970.
32. Evert W. Beth, *Aspects of Modern Logic*. 1970.
33. Risto Hilpinen (ed.), *Deontic Logic: Introductory and Systematic Readings*. 1971.
34. Jean-Louis Krivine, *Introduction to Axiomatic Set Theory*. 1971.
35. Joseph D. Sneed, *The Logical Sstructure of Mathematical Physics*. 1971.
36. Carl R. Kordig, *The Justification of Scientific Change*. 1971.
37. Milic Capek, *Bergson and Modern Physics*. Boston Studies in the Philosophy of Science, Volume VII. 1971.
38. Norwood Russell Hanson, *What I Do Not Believe, and Other Essays* (ed. by Stephen Toulmin and Harry Woolf). 1971.
39. Roger C. Buck and Robert S. Cohen (eds.), *PSA 1970. In Memory of Rudolf Carnap*. Boston Studies in the Philosophy of Science, Volume VIII. 1971.
40. Donald Davidson and Gilbert Harman (eds.), *Semantics of Natural Language*. 1972.
41. Yehoshua Bar-Hillel (ed.), *Pragmatics of Natural Languages*. 1971.
42. Sören Stenlund, *Combinators, λ-Terms and Proof Theory*. 1972.
43. Martin Strauss, *Modern Physics and Its Philosophy. Selected Papers in the Logic, History, and Philosophy of Science*. 1972.
44. Mario Bunge, *Method, Model and Matter*. 1973.
45. Mario Bunge, *Philosophy of Physics*. 1973.
46. A. A. Zinov'ev, *Foundations of the Logical Theory of Scientific Knowledge (Complex Logic)*. (Revised and enlarged English edition with an appendix by G. A. Smirnov, E. A. Sidorenka, A. M. Fedina, and L. A. Bobrova.) Boston Studies in the Philosophy of Science, Volume IX. 1973.
47. Ladislav Tondl, *Scientific Procedures*. Boston Studies in the Philosophy of Science, Volume X. 1973.
48. Norwood Russell Hanson, *Constellations and Conjectures* (ed. by Willard C. Humphreys, Jr.). 1973.

49. K. J. J. Hintikka, J. M. E. Moravcsik, and P. Suppes (eds.), *Approaches to Natural Language.* 1973.
50. Mario Bunge (ed.), *Exact Philosophy – Problems, Tools, and Goals.* 1973.
51. Radu J. Bogdan and Ilkka Niiniluoto (eds.), *Logic, Language, and Probability.* 1973.
52. Glenn Pearce and Patrick Maynard (eds.), *Conceptual Change.* 1973.
53. Ilkka Niiniluoto and Raimo Tuomela, *Theoretical Concepts and Hypothetico-Inductive Inference.* 1973.
54. Roland Fraissé, *Course of Mathematical Logic* – Volume 1: *Relation and Logical Formula.* 1973.
55. Adolf Grünbaum, *Philosophical Problems of Space and Time.* (Second, enlarged edition.) Boston Studies in the Philosophy of Science, Volume XII. 1973.
56. Patrick Suppes (ed.), *Space, Time, and Geometry.* 1973.
57. Hans Kelsen, *Essays in Legal and Moral Philosophy* (selected and introduced by Ota Weinberger). 1973.
58. R. J. Seeger and Robert S. Cohen (eds.), *Philosophical Foundations of Science.* Boston Studies in the Philosophy of Science, Volume XI. 1974.
59. Robert S. Cohen and Marx W. Wartofsky (eds.), *Logical and Epistemological Studies in Contemporary Physics.* Boston Studies in the Philosophy of Science, Volume XIII. 1973.
60. Robert S. Cohen and Marx W. Wartofsky (eds.), *Methodological and Historical Essays in the Natural and Social Sciences. Proceedings of the Boston Colloquium for the Philosophy of Science 1969-1972.* Boston Studies in the Philosophy of Science, Volume XIV. 1974.
61. Robert S. Cohen, J. J. Stachel, and Marx W. Wartofsky (eds.), *For Dirk Struik. Scientific, Historical and Political Essays in Honor of Dirk J. Struik.* Boston Studies in the Philosophy of Science, Volume XV. 1974.
62. Kazimierz Ajdukiewicz, *Pragmatic Logic* (transl. from the Polish by Olgierd Wojtasiewicz). 1974.
63. Sören Stenlund (ed.), *Logical Theory and Semantic Analysis. Essays Dedicated to Stig Kanger on His Fiftieth Birthday.* 1974.
64. Kenneth F. Schaffner and Robert S. Cohen (eds.), *Proceedings of the 1972 Biennial Meeting, Philosophy of Science Association.* Boston Studies in the Philosophy of Science, Volume XX. 1974.
65. Henry E. Kyburg, Jr., *The Logical Foundations of Statistical Inference.* 1974.
66. Marjorie Grene, *The Understanding of Nature. Essays in the Philosophy of Biology.* Boston Studies in the Philosophy of Science, Volume XXIII. 1974.
67. Jan M. Broekman, *Structuralism: Moscow, Prague, Paris.* 1974.
68. Norman Geschwind, *Selected Papers on Language and the Brain.* Boston Studies in the Philosophy of Science, Volume XVI. 1974.
69. Roland Fraissé, *Course of Mathematical Logic* – Volume 2: *Model Theory.* 1974.
70. Andrzej Grzegorczyk, *An Outline of Mathematical Logic. Fundamental Results and Notions Explained with All Details.* 1974.
71. Franz von Kutschera, *Philosophy of Language.* 1975.
72. Juha Manninen and Raimo Tuomela (eds.), *Essays on Explanation and Understanding. Studies in the Foundations of Humanities and Social Sciences.* 1976.

73. Jaakko Hintikka (ed.), *Rudolf Carnap, Logical Empiricist. Materials and Perspectives.* 1975.
74. Milic Capek (ed.), *The Concepts of Space and Time. Their Structure and Their Development.* Boston Studies in the Philosophy of Science, Volume XXII. 1976.
75. Jaakko Hintikka and Unto Remes, *The Method of Analysis. Its Geometrical Origin and Its General Significance.* Boston Studies in the Philosophy of Science, Volume XXV. 1974.
76. John Emery Murdoch and Edith Dudley Sylla, *The Cultural Context of Medieval Learning.* Boston Studies in the Philosophy of Science, Volume XXVI. 1975.
77. Stefan Amsterdamski, *Between Experience and Metaphysics. Philosophical Problems of the Evolution of Science.* Boston Studies in the Philosophy of Science, Volume XXXV. 1975.
78. Patrick Suppes (ed.), *Logic and Probability in Quantum Mechanics.* 1976.
79. Hermann von Helmholtz: *Epistemological Writings. The Paul Hertz/Moritz Schlick Centenary Edition of 1921 with Notes and Commentary by the Editors.* (Newly translated by Malcolm F. Lowe. Edited, with an Introduction and Bibliography, by Robert S. Cohen and Yehuda Elkana.) Boston Studies in the Philosophy of Science, Volume XXXVII. 1977.
80. Joseph Agassi, *Science in Flux.* Boston Studies in the Philosophy of Science, Volume XXVIII. 1975.
81. Sandra G. Harding (ed.), *Can Theories Be Refuted? Essays on the Duhem-Quine Thesis.* 1976.
82. Stefan Nowak, *Methodology of Sociological Research. General Problems.* 1977.
83. Jean Piaget, Jean-Blaise Grize, Alina Szeminska, and Vinh Bang, *Epistemology and Psychology of Functions.* 1977.
84. Marjorie Grene and Everett Mendelsohn (eds.), *Topics in the Philosophy of Biology.* Boston Studies in the Philosophy of Science, Volume XXVII. 1976.
85. E. Fischbein, *The Intuitive Sources of Probabilistic Thinking in Children.* 1975.
86. Ernest W. Adams, *The Logic of Conditionals. An Application of Probability to Deductive Logic.* 1975.
87. Marian Przelecki and Ryszard Wójcicki (eds.), *Twenty-Five Years of Logical Methodology in Poland.* 1977.
88. J. Topolski, *The Methodology of History.* 1976.
89. A. Kasher (ed.), *Language in Focus: Foundations, Methods and Systems. Essays Dedicated to Yehoshua Bar-Hillel.* Boston Studies in the Philosophy of Science, Volume XLIII. 1976.
90. Jaakko Hintikka, *The Intentions of Intentionality and Other New Models for Modalities.* 1975.
91. Wolfgang Stegmüller, *Collected Papers on Epistemology, Philosophy of Science and History of Philosophy.* 2 Volumes. 1977.
92. Dov M. Gabbay, *Investigations in Modal and Tense Logics with Applications to Problems in Philosophy and Linguistics.* 1976.
93. Radu J. Bogdan, *Local Induction.* 1976.
94. Stefan Nowak, *Understanding and Prediction. Essays in the Methodology of Social and Behavioral Theories.* 1976.
95. Peter Mittelstaedt, *Philosophical Problems of Modern Physics.* Boston Studies in the Philosophy of Science, Volume XVIII. 1976.

96. Gerald Holton and William Blanpied (eds.), *Science and Its Public: The Changing Relationship.* Boston Studies in the Philosophy of Science, Volume XXXIII. 1976.
97. Myles Brand and Douglas Walton (eds.), *Action Theory.* 1976.
98. Paul Gochet, *Outline of a Nominalist Theory of Proposition. An Essay in the Theory of Meaning.* 1980. (Forthcoming.)
99. R. S. Cohen, P. K. Feyerabend, and M. W. Wartofsky (eds.), *Essays in Memory of Imre Lakatos.* Boston Studies in the Philosophy of Science, Volume XXXIX. 1976.
100. R. S. Cohen and J. J. Stachel (eds.), *Selected Papers of Léon Rosenfeld.* Boston Studies in the Philosophy of Science, Volume XXI. 1978.
101. R. S. Cohen, C. A. Hooker, A. C. Michalos, and J. W. van Evra (eds.), *PSA 1974: Proceedings of the 1974 Biennial Meeting of the Philosophy of Science Association.* Boston Studies in the Philosophy of Science, Volume XXXII. 1976.
102. Yehuda Fried and Joseph Agassi, *Paranoia: A Study in Diagnosis.* Boston Studies in the Philosophy of Science, Volume L. 1976.
103. Marian Przelecki, Klemens Szaniawski, and Ryszard Wójcicki (eds.), *Formal Methods in the Methodology of Empirical Sciences.* 1976.
104. John M. Vickers, *Belief and Probability.* 1976.
105. Kurt H. Wolff, *Surrender and Catch: Experience and Inquiry Today.* Boston Studies in the Philosophy of Science, Volume LI. 1976.
106. Karel Kosík, *Dialectics of the Concrete.* Boston Studies in the Philosophy of Science, Volume LII. 1976.
107. Nelson Goodman, *The Structure of Appearance.* (Third edition.) Boston Studies in the Philosophy of Science, Volume LIII. 1977.
108. Jerzy Giedymin (ed.), *Kazimierz Ajdukiewicz: The Scientific World-Perspective and Other Essays, 1931-1963.* 1978.
109. Robert L. Causey, *Unity of Science.* 1977.
110. Richard E. Grandy, *Advanced Logic for Applications.* 1977.
111. Robert P. McArthur, *Tense Logic.* 1976.
112. Lars Lindahl, *Position and Change. A Study in Law and Logic.* 1977.
113. Raimo Tuomela, *Dispositions.* 1978.
114 Herbert A. Simon, *Models of Discovery and Other Topics in the Methods of Science.* Boston Studies in the Philosophy of Science, Volume LIV. 1977.
115. Roger D. Rosenkrantz, *Inference, Method and Decision.* 1977.
116. Raimo Tuomela, *Human Action and Its Explanation. A Study on the Philosophical Foundations of Psychology.* 1977.
117. Morris Lazerowitz, *The Language of Philosophy. Freud and Wittgenstein.* Boston Studies in the Philosophy of Science, Volume LV. 1977.
118. Stanislaw Leśniewski, *Collected Works* (ed. by S. J. Surma, J. T. J. Srzednicki, and D. I. Barnett, with an annotated bibliography by V. Frederick Rickey). 1980. (Forthcoming.)
119. Jerzy Pelc, *Semiotics in Poland, 1894-1969.* 1978.
120. Ingmar Pörn, *Action Theory and Social Science. Some Formal Models.* 1977.
121. Joseph Margolis, *Persons and Minds. The Prospects of Nonreductive Materialism.* Boston Studies in the Philosophy of Science, Volume LVII. 1977.
122. Jaakko Hintikka, Ilkka Niiniluoto, and Esa Saarinen (eds.), *Essays on Mathematical and Philosophical Logic.* 1978.
123. Theo A. F. Kuipers, *Studies in Inductive Probability and Rational Expectation.* 1978.

124. Esa Saarinen, Risto Hilpinen, Ilkka Niiniluoto, and Merrill Provence Hintikka (eds.), *Essays in Honour of Jaakko Hintikka on the Occasion of His Fiftieth Birthday*. 1978.

125 Gerard Radnitzky and Gunnar Andersson (eds.), *Progress and Rationality in Science*. Boston Studies in the Philosophy of Science, Volume LVIII. 1978.

126. Peter Mittelstaedt, *Quantum Logic*. 1978.

127. Kenneth A. Bowen, *Model Theory for Modal Logic. Kripke Models for Modal Predicate Calculi*. 1978.

128. Howard Alexander Bursen, *Dismantling the Memory Machine. A Philosophical Investigation of Machine Theories of Memory*. 1978.

129. Marx W. Wartofsky, *Models: Representation and the Scientific Understanding*. Boston Studies in the Philosophy of Science, Volume XLVIII. 1979.

130. Don Ihde, *Technics and Praxis. A Philosophy of Technology*. Boston Studies in the Philosophy of Science, Volume XXIV. 1978.

131. Jerzy J. Wiatr (ed.), *Polish Essays in the Methodology of the Social Sciences*. Boston Studies in the Philosophy of Science, Volume XXIX. 1979.

132. Wesley C. Salmon (ed.), *Hans Reichenbach: Logical Empiricist*. 1979.

133. Peter Bieri, Rolf-P. Horstmann, and Lorenz Krüger (eds.), *Transcendental Arguments in Science. Essays in Epistemology*. 1979.

134. Mihailo Marković and Gajo Petrović (eds.), *Praxis. Yugoslav Essays in the Philosophy and Methodology of the Social Sciences*. Boston Studies in the Philosophy of Science, Volume XXXVI. 1979.

135. Ryszard Wójcicki, *Topics in the Formal Methodology of Empirical Sciences*. 1979.

136. Gerard Radnitzky and Gunnar Andersson (eds.), *The Structure and Development of Science*. Boston Studies in the Philosophy of Science, Volume LIX. 1979.

137. Judson Chambers Webb, *Mechanism, Mentalism, and Metamathematics. An Essay on Finitism*. 1980. (Forthcoming.)

138. D. F. Gustafson and B. L. Tapscott (eds.), *Body, Mind, and Method. Essays in Honor of Virgil C. Aldrich*. 1979.

139. Leszek Nowak, *The Structure of Idealization. Towards a Systematic Interpretation of the Marxian Idea of Science*. 1979.

140. Chaim Perelman, *The New Rhetoric and the Humanities. Essays on Rhetoric and Its Applications*. 1979.

141. Wlodzimierz Rabinowicz, *Universalizability. A Study in Morals and Metaphysics*. 1979.